GCSE English

Lord of the Flies

by William Golding

Lord of the Flies is a terrifying trip into the dark hearts of schoolboys
— and it's a tough book to write GCSE essays about too.

Not to worry. This brilliant Text Guide explains the whole thing —
characters, language, themes, historical background... the lot. And because
it's a CGP book, we get straight to the point, with no needless rambling.

We've also included plenty of practice questions to test you on what you've
learned, plus advice on how to plan and write top-grade answers in the exam!
You'll be Lord of the Fly Swots in no time.

The Text Guide

CONTENTS

Introduction

Introducing 'Lord of the Flies' and William Golding..1
Background Information 2
Who's Who in 'Lord of the Flies' 3
'Lord of the Flies' — Plot Summary 4

Section One — Discussion of Chapters

Chapter One Analysis — The Sound of the Shell 6
Chapter Two Analysis — Fire on the Mountain...7
Chapter Three Analysis — Huts on the Beach...8
Chapter Four Analysis — Painted Faces and Long Hair 9
Chapter Five Analysis — Beast from Water 10
Chapter Six Analysis — Beast from Air 11
Chapter Seven Analysis — Shadows and Tall Trees 12
Chapter Eight Analysis — Gift for the Darkness..13
Chapter Nine Analysis — A View to a Death 14
Chapter Ten Analysis — The Shell and the Glasses 15
Chapter Eleven Analysis — Castle Rock 16
Chapter Twelve Analysis — Cry of the Hunters...17
Practice Questions 18

Section Two — Characters

Character Profile — Ralph 20
Character Profile — Piggy 22
Character Profile — Jack 24
Character Profile — Simon...26
Character Profile — Roger 28
Character Profile — The Littluns..29
Character Profile — The Other Characters...30
Practice Questions 31

CONTENTS

Section Three — Themes

Civilisation and Barbarity..34
Fear 36
Power and Leadership..37
Nature 38
Games 39
Evil 40
Practice Questions 41

Section Four — The Writer's Techniques

Structure and Viewpoint of 'Lord of the Flies'..................................43
How the Characters Speak 44
Imagery and Symbolism..45
Practice Questions 46

Section Five — Background and Context

Historical Background to 'Lord of the Flies'.....................................48
Adventure Stories..50
Practice Questions 51

Section Six — Exam Advice

Exam Preparation..53
The Exam Question..54
Planning Your Answer 55
Writing Introductions and Conclusions 56
Writing Main Paragraphs...57
In the Exam...58
Sample Exam Question 59
Worked Answer 60

Index 62
The Characters from 'Lord of the Flies'
'Lord of the Flies' Cartoon

Published by CGP

Editors:
Claire Boulter
Alex Fairer
Rebecca Tate

Contributors:
Samantha Bensted
Holly Corfield-Carr
Nicola Woodfin

With thanks to Luke von Kotze and Nicola Woodfin for the proofreading.

Acknowledgements:

With thanks to Lilith Antinori, National Geographic and John Stanmeyer/VII for permission to use the front cover image.

With thanks to Mary Evans Picture Library for permission to use the images on pages 1, 2 and 49.

With thanks to Rex Features for permission to use the images on pages 1, 39, 44, 45 and 48.

With thanks to Alamy for permission to use the images on pages 3, 4, 5, 6, 8, 11, 13, 14, 15, 16, 20, 22, 24, 25, 28, 29, 30, 35, 36 and 37.

Images on pages 3, 4, 5 and 26 Lord of the Flies © 1990 Castle Rock Entertainment. All Rights Reserved.

Images on pages 3, 7, 10, 12, 34 and 40 from the 1963 Lord of the Flies film Courtesy of Janus Films.

With thanks to iStockphoto.com for permission to use the images on pages 5, 9, 27, 38 and 43.

With thanks to TopFoto for permission to use the image on page 17 © 1999 Topham Picturepoint

Every effort has been made to locate copyright holders and obtain permission to reproduce sources.
For those sources where it has been difficult to trace the copyright holder of the work, we would be grateful
for information. If any copyright holder would like us to make an amendment to the acknowledgements,
please notify us and we will gladly update the book at the next reprint. Thank you.

For copyright reasons, this book is not for sale in the USA or Canada.

ISBN: 978 1 84762 022 4
Printed by Bell & Bain Ltd, Glasgow.
Clipart from Corel®

Based on the classic CGP style created by Richard Parsons.

Introducing 'Lord of the Flies' and William Golding

'Lord of the Flies' is about the dark side of human nature

- *Lord of the Flies* is about a group of boys who are <u>stranded</u> on a tropical <u>island</u>.

- The boys <u>change</u> from <u>civilised public schoolboys</u> into <u>savages</u> —
  this mirrors the struggle between <u>good</u> and <u>evil</u> in all humans.

Lord of the Flies has a strong message

1) Golding believed that <u>evil</u> exists inside <u>everyone</u> and is only contained by the rules of <u>society</u>.

2) He thought that, under the right <u>conditions</u>, evil could come to the <u>surface</u> and 'normal' people could commit <u>terrible crimes</u>.

© Interfoto / Sammlung Rauch / Mary Evans

William Golding was deeply affected by his experience of war

- Golding wrote *Lord of the Flies* in the <u>1950s</u> — a few years after the end of <u>World War Two</u>.

- Golding was shocked by the <u>horrors</u> of World War Two, which he realised were carried out "<u>coldly</u>" and "<u>skilfully</u>" by <u>educated</u> people who came from a "<u>tradition of civilisation</u>".

- Although the <u>Nazis</u> were defeated, he believed that similar evil could <u>resurface</u> at any time.

1911	Born in <u>Newquay</u>, Cornwall.
1935	Started a career in <u>teaching</u>.
1939-45	<u>World War Two</u>. Golding joined the <u>Royal Navy</u> in 1940. He was involved in the <u>D-Day invasion</u> of Normandy.
1945	Left the Navy and returned to teaching.
1954	'<u>Lord of the Flies</u>' was published.
1962	Retired from teaching to become a <u>full-time writer</u>.
1983	Won the <u>Nobel Prize in Literature</u>.
1988	<u>Knighted</u> by the Queen.
1993	Died, aged 81.

© Nick Rogers/Rex Features

2

Background Information

'Lord of the Flies' is set on a tropical island in the Pacific Ocean

Here's a map of the island, showing where all the important action happens.

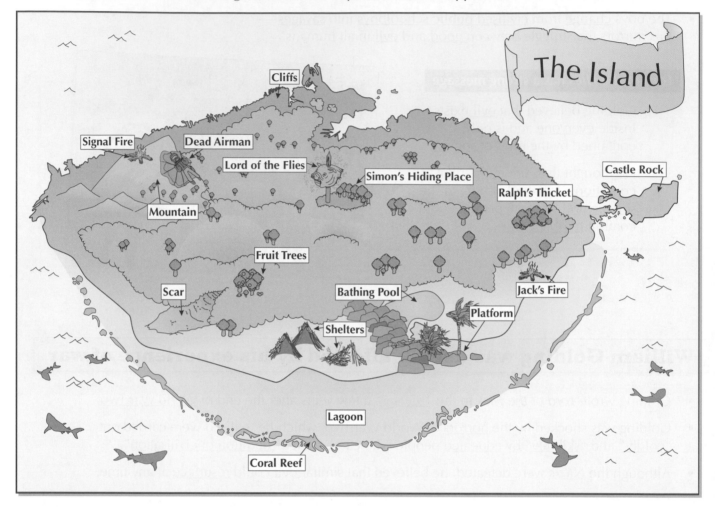

Golding's teaching experience helped him write 'Lord of the Flies'

© Country Life / IPC Media / Mary Evans

- William Golding taught boys in private schools for many years before he wrote *Lord of the Flies*. He later wrote that he understood young boys with "awful precision".

- He believed that adventure stories like *The Coral Island* were unrealistic in their optimistic view of how young boys would act without adult supervision or rules.

- He wanted to write an adventure story that showed more accurately how children would behave without rules.

Who's Who in 'Lord of the Flies'

Ralph...
...is elected by the boys as their leader. He tries to stick to values of decency and fair play.

© Moviestore collection Ltd / Alamy

Jack...
...is Ralph's main rival. He becomes obsessed with hunting. He rebels against Ralph.

© Moviestore collection Ltd / Alamy

Piggy...
...is overweight, wears glasses and has asthma. He's intelligent — but is seen as an outsider.

© Photos 12 / Alamy

Simon...
...is kind and shy. There's something spiritual about him and he's often alone.

Courtesy of MGM Media Licensing

© Moviestore collection Ltd / Alamy

Roger...
...is cruel and nasty. He enjoys inflicting pain on people and animals.

The 'littluns'...
...are the youngest kids. The older boys don't look after them very well.

© AF archive / Alamy

Sam and Eric...
...are identical twins. They stay loyal to Ralph until they're forced to join Jack's tribe.

© Photos 12 / Alamy

Courtesy of Janus Films

The 'Lord of the Flies'...
...is a pig's head on a stick that represents the evil inside all of the characters.

'Lord of the Flies' — Plot Summary

'Lord of the Flies'... what happens when?

Lord of the Flies needs to be as familiar to you as your favourite socks. This little recap of the main events will help you on your way, but it's no substitute for reading the book. There's no escaping that I'm afraid...

Chapters One to Three — exploring the island

- A group of schoolboys are stranded on an island after a plane crash. There are no adults.

- They have a meeting and Ralph is elected chief, but Jack also wanted the job.

- Ralph, Jack and Simon explore. Jack nearly kills a piglet, but he hesitates and it escapes.

- The younger boys ('littluns') are afraid of a beast that one of them thinks he saw at night.

- Ralph uses Piggy's glasses to light a fire to signal ships. The boys are excited by the fire at first, but it gets out of control and a littlun is killed.

- Ralph spends all his time building shelters with Simon — he gets angry that all Jack and the other older boys do is hunt. Ralph and Jack argue, then make up. Simon goes off into the forest to be by himself.

Chapters Four to Six — hunting for food and tracking the beast

- Ralph, Simon and Piggy see a ship, but Jack has taken all the boys hunting and let the signal fire go out. The ship disappears without noticing them.

- The hunters come back chanting, with a pig that Jack has killed.

- Ralph and Jack argue about the fire. Jack hits Piggy, breaking his glasses.

- They act out the hunt — Maurice pretends to be the pig while they dance and chant.

- The boys hold a meeting to discuss their fears.

- A dead airman lands on the island. Sam and Eric see the body in the dark and panic. They tell the others they've seen the beast.

- The boys hunt the beast, and find Castle Rock.

Introduction

Chapters Seven to Nine — the group splits

- Ralph <u>injures</u> a pig while hunting. The boys re-enact the hunt and Robert is slightly <u>hurt</u>.

- Ralph, Roger and Jack climb the <u>mountain</u> in the dark and see the <u>dead airman</u>. They think it's the <u>beast</u>.

- Jack tries to get elected as <u>chief</u> but fails. He forms his own <u>tribe</u> and boys gradually <u>join</u> him, until only Ralph, Piggy, Sam, Eric and the littluns are <u>left</u>.

- Jack's tribe <u>viciously kills</u> a pig. They put its <u>head</u> on a stick as a gift for the beast.

- Simon finds the pig's <u>head</u> covered in flies — the <u>Lord of the Flies</u>. He thinks it's <u>talking</u> to him. He finds the <u>dead airman</u> and goes back to tell the others what the <u>beast</u> really is.

- Ralph and Piggy go to Jack's feast and <u>join in</u> the tribe's <u>hunting dance</u>. Simon stumbles into the <u>middle</u> of the dance. The tribe thinks that he's the beast and <u>kills</u> him.

Courtesy of MGM Media Licensing

Chapters Ten to Twelve — Jack turns against Ralph's group

- Jack's tribe <u>attack</u> Ralph's group and steal Piggy's <u>glasses</u> so they can light a <u>fire</u>.

© Pictorial Press Ltd / Alamy

- Ralph's group tries to get Piggy's <u>glasses</u> back but Sam and Eric are <u>captured</u>. Roger levers a <u>rock</u> off the cliff, which <u>kills</u> Piggy.

- The <u>tribe</u> begins to <u>hunt</u> Ralph and he <u>runs</u> into the forest to <u>hide</u>. He finds the Lord of the Flies and <u>destroys</u> it.

- Jack's tribe rolls <u>boulders</u> at the thicket Ralph's hiding in, then lights a <u>fire</u> to smoke him out.

- Ralph <u>runs</u> away and the tribe <u>chases</u> him. He runs into a <u>naval officer</u> whose ship saw the <u>smoke</u> from Jack's fire. The boys <u>start crying</u>.

Simon says — keep reading, or I'll set Jack on you...

On the surface, *Lord of the Flies* is an adventure story about a group of boys stranded on an island, but it also has a deeper message about the evil that's inside everyone. Once you've got your head round that, move on to Section One. If you're still unsure about the novel's plot or want a break from revision, have a look at the *Lord of the Flies* cartoon on p.64.

© iStockphoto.com / Steve Geer

Chapter One Analysis — The Sound of the Shell

The book is about a group of schoolboys, stranded on a remote island. If this is all you know about it, it's probably a good idea to read the handy plot summary on p.4-5 — it'll fill you in on what happens when.

The boys gather together after a plane crash

1) <u>Ralph</u> comes out of the jungle onto the <u>beach</u>, followed by <u>Piggy</u>.

2) The two boys find a <u>conch</u> shell. <u>Piggy</u> knows what the conch is, and has the idea of using it to <u>call</u> the others. This suggests he's <u>intelligent</u>.

3) A bunch of choirboys arrive <u>marching</u> in step — they're already a <u>group</u> <u>of their own</u>. They're described as "<u>something dark</u>", which hints that there may be an <u>evil</u> side to them.

4) There aren't any <u>grown-ups</u> on the island — the boys are <u>excited</u>, but they're not <u>sure</u> how to <u>behave</u>.

Theme — Civilisation and Barbarity

Piggy mentions an "<u>atom bomb</u>" and says that the adults are "<u>all dead</u>". The outside world is <u>war-torn</u> and <u>violent</u>.

© Pictorial Press Ltd / Alamy

This chapter is mainly optimistic...

Theme — Nature

Golding uses <u>descriptive language</u> to give the reader an idea of the <u>beauty</u> of the novel's <u>setting</u> — the island. It has a shore "<u>fledged</u> with palm trees", and a lagoon of "<u>shimmering</u> water". It's a paradise, like the <u>Garden of Eden</u> (see p.38).

1) <u>Ralph</u> is <u>elected</u> as chief. Everyone accepts the decision — <u>even Jack</u> who wanted to be the leader himself. So far, they're sticking to the <u>rules</u> of their <u>old life</u> and trying to <u>re-create</u> the <u>society</u> they're used to.

2) The boys feel <u>excited</u> as they go exploring, and <u>triumphant</u> when they reach the top of the mountain. They've <u>conquered</u> the island — it "belongs" to them.

...but there are hints of the conflict and danger to come

1) Jack's <u>humiliated</u> when Ralph is chosen as chief instead of him. This suggests there might be <u>tension</u> between the two boys <u>later</u> in the story.

2) Jack's frustrated when he <u>fails</u> to kill a piglet that they find <u>trapped</u> in a creeper. This is the beginning of the <u>obsession</u> with hunting that <u>splits</u> the group later on.

3) The <u>descriptions</u> of the island aren't all <u>friendly</u> — the heat is a "<u>threatening weight</u>", the coconuts are "skull-like" and Piggy's knees get "<u>scratched</u> by thorns". Golding is <u>hinting</u> that their time on the island won't all be <u>fun</u> and <u>adventure</u>.

4) The boys <u>bully Piggy</u> — it's <u>cruel</u>, but still '<u>acceptable behaviour</u>' according to the <u>rules</u> of their old lives. This sets Piggy up as an <u>outsider</u> who's <u>different</u> from the others.

KEY QUOTE

"Next time there would be no mercy."

Jack can't kill the pig because of the "enormity of the knife descending and cutting into living flesh". He's still kind of civilised — but his promise to kill next time hints at how he'll soon become more savage.

Chapter Two Analysis — Fire on the Mountain

At the beginning of Chapter Two, everything is ticking over nicely... but by the end it's clear that this story isn't going to be all fun and games and making loud noises by blowing shells (as much fun as that sounds).

The boys establish rules

1) Ralph sets out <u>rules</u> for the boys, <u>based</u> on school rules — like "Hands up" and taking it in <u>turns</u> to speak. He's trying to <u>maintain</u> the <u>civilised behaviour</u> of their old lives.

Symbolism
Golding introduces the <u>conch</u> as a symbol of <u>democracy</u> — it's linked to <u>Ralph's leadership</u>.

Theme — Power and Leadership
Ralph wants <u>rules</u> to <u>allow</u> the boys to live together <u>fairly</u>. Jack sees them as a way of <u>controlling</u> the other boys.

2) Jack's <u>excited</u> about having <u>rules</u> because he wants to <u>punish</u> anyone who <u>breaks</u> them. This gives the reader an <u>idea</u> of what <u>kind</u> of <u>leader</u> he'd be.

The election and the idea of having a chief are games that the boys are playing.

There are the first signs of fear

1) Piggy says they might be on the island for <u>a long time</u>. This <u>frightens</u> the boys, but they quickly <u>dismiss</u> the fear, and plan to "<u>have fun</u>" until they're rescued.

2) A <u>littlun</u> says he saw a <u>snake-like beast</u> in the night.

- Ralph tries to explain that the beast <u>doesn't exist</u>, but it's not easy to <u>persuade</u> the others — their irrational fear is "<u>ungraspable</u>". This is a reminder that the characters are just <u>children</u>, so their <u>fear</u> could get <u>out of control</u>.

- Jack says he'll "look for the <u>snake</u>" when he's <u>hunting</u> — he's <u>undermining</u> Ralph's authority and using the littluns' fear to make himself more <u>powerful</u>.

Courtesy of Janus Films

They get carried away building a signal fire

1) As soon as Ralph suggests building a <u>signal fire</u>, the <u>rules are forgotten</u> — the boys' desire to have <u>fun</u> is stronger than their <u>respect</u> for the rules.

2) The fire gets <u>out of control</u>. It burns up all their <u>firewood</u> and <u>kills</u> a <u>littlun</u>.

3) The boys are <u>shocked</u> and <u>ashamed</u> when they realise what's happened — they <u>still</u> have the <u>moral values</u> that <u>civilised society</u> has taught them.

4) This death happens because they're <u>careless</u>, but it changes the <u>atmosphere</u> of the novel from one of <u>excited adventure</u>, to one of <u>serious danger</u>. It's a hint that this isn't a classic <u>adventure story</u> (see p.50).

Symbolism
The <u>signal fire</u> is a <u>symbol</u> of the boys' <u>hope</u> that they'll be <u>rescued</u>.

EXAM TIP

Write about the conflict between civilisation and savagery...
You can write about how quickly this conflict emerges in Chapter Two. The boys try to introduce rules and act in a civilised way, but instead they get excited by fire and accidentally kill someone. Not a great start...

Chapter Three Analysis — Huts on the Beach

Ralph and Jack are already starting to have minor disagreements — who left the toilet seat up, who put the empty milk carton back in the fridge, whether savagely slaughtering pigs is really necessary — the usual stuff...

Jack sends the hunters away and hunts alone

1) Jack's <u>determined</u> to kill a pig. He's ditched his <u>school uniform</u> and only wears shorts and "a knife-belt". His <u>hair</u> has grown <u>longer</u> and he carries a <u>sharp stick</u>. He's <u>losing</u> his old, <u>public-schoolboy identity</u>.

2) Jack throws his <u>spear</u> at a pig but <u>misses</u>. He's no longer <u>held back</u> by the rules of his <u>old life</u> which <u>stopped</u> him from <u>killing the piglet</u> in Chapter One. He's becoming less <u>civilised</u> and more <u>savage</u>.

The differences between Jack and Ralph get more obvious

1) Jack and Ralph <u>argue</u> about their <u>different priorities</u>. Ralph thinks they should focus on building <u>shelters</u> to be a "Home" for the boys, and keeping the <u>signal fire</u> going — Jack's only interested in <u>killing a pig</u>.

2) Golding uses the <u>tension</u> between <u>Ralph</u> and <u>Jack</u> to symbolise the tension between <u>civilisation</u> and <u>barbarity</u> in every person.

3) The argument blows over — but <u>only just</u>. They can't <u>understand</u> each other — they look at each other "<u>baffled</u>, in love and hate".

4) Jack has to <u>think</u> before he <u>remembers</u> what rescue is — he's <u>forgetting</u> his old life.

© Pictorial Press Ltd / Alamy

Theme — Civilisation and Barbarity

Jack <u>justifies</u> his desire to hunt by saying it's for <u>everyone's benefit</u> — "we want <u>meat</u>". Later on, he no longer tries to justify it — he just does it because he <u>wants to</u>. This shows the changing balance between <u>civilisation</u> (where people look after each other) and <u>savagery</u> (where everyone looks after himself).

Simon goes off on his own into the forest

1) Simon <u>helps</u> the littluns by picking fruit that's too high for them — this shows his <u>kindness</u>. He provides them with <u>food</u> — just as Jack promised to. Unlike Jack, he <u>doesn't</u> expect <u>gratitude</u> or <u>obedience</u> in return.

2) He finds a <u>quiet</u> spot in the forest and sits <u>alone</u>. The scene has a <u>spiritual</u> atmosphere — it suggests Simon is <u>different</u> from the others.

3) Simon wears "the <u>remains</u> of shorts" and his "feet were <u>bare</u>" — quite a long <u>time</u> has passed since the boys arrived.

Theme — Nature

Jack goes off to <u>hunt</u> and <u>kill</u>, but Simon is at one with <u>nature</u>, and <u>blends in</u> with his surroundings.

"All the same, I'd like to catch a pig first"

This chapter sets the scene for some major disagreements later on. Ralph's focused on trying to get them all rescued, but Jack seems more interested in slaughtering a pig. Honestly — priorities, Jack, priorities.

Chapter Four Analysis — Painted Faces and Long Hair

Jack and Ralph continue to argue in Chapter Four, only this time, things get a bit more serious. You can see Ralph's point though — if I was stranded on an island with this lot, I'd rather get rescued than eat a bit of meat.

Violence begins to creep in

1) Roger and Maurice <u>kick over</u> the littluns' sand castles. Maurice is still <u>civilised</u> enough to feel "the unease of wrong-doing", and he leaves feeling <u>ashamed</u>.

Theme — Games

<u>Destructive games</u> turn into <u>dangerous hunts</u> later in the novel.

Theme — Nature

The boys are now <u>used</u> to life on the <u>island</u>, but they're not <u>happy</u> or <u>safe</u> — the heat is "a <u>blow</u>" and they're "<u>menaced</u> by the coming of dark".

2) Roger throws <u>stones</u> around a littlun, but he doesn't try to hit him. He's been "<u>conditioned</u>" by society not to hurt others — but his <u>excitement</u> shows that he <u>wants</u> to.

3) Jack paints a <u>mask</u> onto his face which turns him into an "<u>awesome stranger</u>" — he's "<u>liberated from shame</u>" and could be <u>capable of anything</u>.

The boys have a chance of rescue — but the fire is out

KEY EVENT

1) Ralph, Simon and Piggy see a <u>ship</u> — but Jack's taken everyone <u>hunting</u> and let the <u>fire go out</u>.

2) The boys are losing sight of the <u>reason</u> for keeping the <u>fire</u> going — their desire to <u>hunt</u> is starting to take over from their desire to be <u>rescued</u>.

3) The hunters are <u>upset</u> when they realise what's happened — they haven't <u>completely forgotten</u> their old lives.

Turning point in the action
The fire going out brings the tension between Ralph and Jack into the open.

© iStockphoto.com / Luke Daniek

The conflict between Ralph and Jack becomes violent

1) Jack feels <u>ashamed</u> about the fire — he takes his <u>frustration</u> out by hitting Piggy, <u>breaking</u> his <u>glasses</u> — it's a sign that Piggy's <u>logical</u> way of thinking is about to become <u>less important</u>.

Symbolism

The <u>fire</u> symbolises <u>civilisation</u>, and <u>hunting</u> symbolises <u>savagery</u> — they're in <u>direct conflict</u> here.

Theme — Civilisation and Barbarity

They re-enact the <u>hunt</u>, and Maurice pretends to be a pig. The <u>line</u> between violence towards <u>animals</u> and towards <u>humans</u> is becoming <u>blurred</u>.

2) Jack <u>apologises</u> for letting the fire go out, and hands out <u>meat</u>. Earning the boys' <u>respect</u> and <u>providing</u> food for them helps him <u>take control</u>. It foreshadows the way he <u>takes power</u> later.

3) Ralph announces that he's calling an <u>assembly</u>. He still trusts the <u>authority</u> the conch gives him to enforce the <u>old rules</u>.

EXAM TIP

Write about how Golding uses language to show savagery...

The hunters chant "*Kill the pig. Cut her throat. Spill her blood.*" This simplistic, violent language shows how they're becoming less civilised. In fact, this chant would be a handy quote to revise for your exam.

Chapter Five Analysis — Beast from Water

By Chapter Five the island is in a pretty bad way — the fire's gone out, no one's helping to build the shelters, their clothes are falling apart, there's poo everywhere, and worst of all — they all need a decent haircut...

Ralph realises things are going wrong

1) Ralph begins to <u>realise</u> his own <u>failings</u> and doubt his <u>ability</u> to be chief. His <u>dirty uniform</u> and <u>long hair</u> make him realise how far from civilisation the boys have slipped.

2) He calls a <u>meeting</u> to remind the boys of the <u>rules</u> — they're beginning to <u>ignore</u> them and to descend into <u>savagery</u>.

Symbolism

The <u>shelters</u> represent <u>civilisation</u> — all the boys helped build the first one, and it's <u>sturdy</u>, but the one which only Ralph and Simon built is "<u>tottery</u>". Without all the boys <u>working together</u> and agreeing, society <u>doesn't work</u>.

Courtesy of Janus Films

The beast divides the group

1) Ralph sees that <u>fear</u> of the beast is <u>damaging</u> the group and wants them to "decide there's <u>nothing</u> in it". Piggy thinks that the <u>only</u> thing to fear is <u>people</u>, and Simon suggests that the beast is actually <u>themselves</u>. Nobody takes either of them <u>seriously</u>.

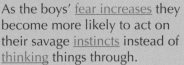

Theme — Fear

As the boys' <u>fear increases</u> they become more likely to act on their savage <u>instincts</u> instead of <u>thinking</u> things through.

2) Jack calls the littluns "<u>cry-babies and sissies</u>" for being frightened of the beast. He says it <u>doesn't exist</u>, but then says "<u>we'll hunt it down!</u>" This makes the beast seem more <u>real</u>, and makes hunting seem <u>necessary</u> for the boys' <u>safety</u>. This gives Jack <u>more power</u>.

3) Phil <u>mistakes</u> Simon for the <u>beast</u> — this <u>foreshadows</u> Simon's <u>murder</u> later in the novel.

The rules of the conch are becoming less important

1) Jack speaks <u>without the conch</u> and Piggy and Simon are <u>shouted down</u> even when they have it.

2) Ralph tells Jack that "the rules are the <u>only thing</u> we've got" — the only thing that ties them to <u>civilisation</u>, but Jack replies "<u>Bollocks to the rules!</u>" His emphasis on <u>having fun</u> and hunting the beast appeals to the other boys' <u>growing savagery</u>.

3) Jack takes advantage of the <u>chaos</u> caused by the boys' <u>fear</u> of the beast, and <u>excitement</u> about hunting it, to gain <u>power</u> — he breaks up the assembly to stage a <u>mock hunt</u>.

Theme — Civilisation and Barbarity

Only Ralph, Piggy and Simon are left — there's a clear <u>separation</u> between the boys who value <u>civilisation</u> and <u>logic</u>, and those who have let their <u>fear</u> turn them into <u>savages</u>.

4) Ralph <u>doesn't</u> blow the <u>conch</u> to call the boys back — he's afraid they'll <u>ignore</u> it and see he's <u>losing</u> his authority. He realises that <u>Jack's</u> becoming more <u>powerful</u>.

KEY QUOTE *"What I mean is... maybe it's only us."*
Simon hits the nail on the head when he suggests that the beast is themselves — he realises that everybody has evil inside them. If only the others had listened to him. They might've had a jolly, savagery-free time.

Chapter Six Analysis — Beast from Air

When the "beast" finally arrives, it's not a real beast at all. It's just a rotting, fly-smothered, foul-smelling, rancid dead body that makes weird noises and moves in the wind in a lifelike way. Not scary at all then...

The body of a dead airman lands on the island

1) While everyone is asleep, a <u>dead airman</u> parachutes down from an aircraft <u>battle</u> above the island. It's a <u>reminder</u> of the <u>war</u> going on in the outside world.

Turning point in the action
Most of the boys now believe the beast is real.

> The <u>dead airman</u> is the <u>sign</u> from the <u>adult</u> world that the boys <u>asked</u> for.

2) Sam and Eric <u>spot</u> the dead parachutist and think he's the <u>beast</u>. They <u>exaggerate</u> their story and give the boys a <u>real beast</u> to focus their <u>fears</u> on.

Ralph and Jack have different plans to deal with the beast

1) Ralph wants to <u>think</u> things through, but Jack wants to track the beast <u>immediately</u>. He says "This is a <u>hunter's</u> job" — he uses the beast to <u>gain power</u>.

2) The boys' <u>fear</u> of the <u>beast</u> is more immediate than their desire to be <u>rescued</u> — this tips the <u>balance</u> in favour of <u>Jack's</u> leadership. Ralph only <u>keeps</u> his leadership by agreeing to <u>hunt</u>.

Theme — Fear
Jack <u>forces</u> Ralph to hunt the beast by suggesting that he's <u>afraid</u>.

© Moviestore collection Ltd / Alamy

Theme — Power and Leadership
Ralph is <u>terrified</u> of going first when they get to Castle Rock, but <u>forces</u> himself to because that's what the <u>chief</u> should do. He knows he needs to seem <u>brave</u> to stop Jack <u>taking over</u> as leader.

Jack and Ralph feel differently about Castle Rock

1) The two boys' <u>reactions</u> to Castle Rock reflect their <u>leadership styles</u> and how <u>civilised</u> or <u>savage</u> they are.

2) Jack thinks it would be a good place for a <u>fort</u>, and he imagines defending it from <u>enemies</u>. It suits his <u>aggressive</u> leadership style and his urge towards <u>savagery</u>.

Theme — Games
The game of <u>rolling boulders</u> is developed here. Jack gets the idea to <u>push</u> a rock onto the "<u>narrow causeway</u>" if an "<u>enemy</u>" comes. This <u>foreshadows</u> Piggy's death in Chapter Eleven.

Theme — Power and Leadership
When Ralph asks the boys to relight the signal fire, they <u>obey</u> him "<u>mutinously</u>" — he's losing <u>authority</u> all the time now.

3) Ralph thinks it's a "<u>rotten place</u>" to set up a base. There's no <u>food</u> or <u>shelter</u> and not much fresh <u>water</u>. Golding is showing the reader that Ralph's civilised values are more <u>sensible</u> than Jack's savage ones.

Comment on Golding's use of foreshadowing...
It's good to mention how Golding hints at what's to come later in the novel — Jack's thoughts about defending Castle Rock and rolling boulders onto "an enemy" become more than just a fantasy (see p.16).

Chapter Seven Analysis — Shadows and Tall Trees

Ralph's position doesn't seem to be as secure as it was — his authority is slipping away from him. So now it's time for him to try to prove that he's just as brave and strong as Jack. Not that he's competitive or anything...

Ralph feels trapped on the island

1) While they're looking for the beast, Ralph gets a sense of the "remoteness of the sea", and begins to think of it as "the barrier" that keeps them away from civilisation. He feels "helpless" and "condemned".

2) Golding uses this descriptive language to show how alone and cut off from the civilised world the boys are.

3) Simon's prophecy that Ralph will get back home helps Ralph get control of himself and carry on. It also reminds the reader that there's something spiritual about Simon (see p.27).

> **Theme — Nature**
>
> At first, Golding described the novel's setting as a tropical paradise. Now the island has become a prison, trapping the boys with each other.

Ralph joins the pig hunt

> **Theme — Power and Leadership**
>
> Jack puts Ralph down by saying he threw badly. He sees himself as the leader of the hunt and can't stand Ralph challenging his power.

1) Ralph gets carried away while hunting a pig, and he begins to understand how appealing hunting can be. He feels that he's earned a "new respect" after wounding the pig.

> **Theme — Civilisation and Barbarity**
>
> Ralph's involvement in the hunt and the re-enactment is a further step towards savagery and a hint that Jack's violent leadership will soon replace Ralph's civilised morals.

2) The boys re-enact the hunt, and even Ralph joins in. It gets out of hand and only ends when Jack pretends to kill Robert. Ralph "uneasily" reminds himself that it was "just a game". When Robert suggests using a pig next time because they've "got to kill him", Jack jokes that they should "Use a littlun".

Ralph and Jack struggle for control of the group

1) Ralph wants to wait until morning to climb the mountain, but Jack challenges him, suggesting he's "frightened". Neither of them wants to look like a coward in front of the others.

2) Their struggle for power overcomes their fear of the beast and they go up the mountain with Roger. They see the dead airman — in the dark they mistake him for the beast.

> **Theme — Fear**
>
> It's the boys' fear of looking like cowards that makes them go up the mountain in the dark. If they'd waited for light they'd have seen the dead airman, not the beast. Golding is showing that the beast is a reflection of their own fear and savagery.

Courtesy of Janus Films

Make sure you discuss Golding's message...

Golding is saying that everyone and anyone is capable of savagery. Ralph has been the voice of civilisation so far in the novel, but in this chapter he discovers that he likes hunting too, nicely illustrating Golding's point.

Chapter Eight Analysis — Gift for the Darkness

In Chapter Eight, Jack has the mother of all hissy fits. If only they had a kettle, some tea bags and a splash of milk on the island, they could settle their differences over a nice cup of tea...

Jack tries to take over as chief

1) Jack tries to seize power from Ralph, blowing the conch and calling another election. He loses, but secretly boys begin to join his tribe.

2) Jack uses the boys' certainty that the beast exists to gain power — they believe Jack and his hunters can deal with the beast.

3) Ralph dismisses the hunters as "Boys armed with sticks". His words are similar to Golding's description of the boys from the naval officer's point of view in Chapter Twelve — "little boys" carrying "sharp sticks". This shows that Ralph sees them from an adult point of view.

Theme — Power and Leadership

Jack uses the conch to try to get power from Ralph. When he can't take over as chief, he abandons democracy and sets himself up as a dictator.

Jack's new group viciously kills a pig

Turning point in the action
Jack seizes power without a vote.

1) Jack declares himself leader of the new group, saying "I'm going to be chief." The other boys don't question this — they no longer expect democracy.

2) They slaughter a pig, laughing at the blood and smearing it on their faces. They find violence funny — this contrasts with Jack's failure to kill the piglet in Chapter One.

Symbolism

Ralph's group stays by the homely shelters, while Jack's group sets up camp on the wild, unfriendly side of the island — this reflects their different values.

3) Jack leaves the pig's head for the beast. This shows how Jack's tribe are starting to act based on superstition rather than reason.

© AF archive / Alamy

Simon finds the pig's head — the Lord of the Flies

KEY EVENT

Theme — Nature

Golding usually describes Simon's experiences of nature as beautiful and spiritual, but here he sees the dark, dirty, brutal side of nature.

1) Simon's terrified of the Lord of the Flies — he sees that it represents the evil inside everyone, and he's afraid that it's in him too.

2) He has a choice — he could accept his savage side and "have fun" with the others, or he could ignore the Lord of the Flies's threat that "we shall do you" and try to stop their slide into savagery. He chooses to warn the others — this shows his bravery and goodness.

KEY QUOTE *"I'm not going to play any longer. Not with you."*
Jack's language here emphasises that he's still a child — this makes his savagery even more shocking. Then again, he does have a rather impressive skill set. I mean, can Ralph sing C sharp? I think not.

Chapter Nine Analysis — A View to a Death

Once Jack's tribe start their weird dancing and chanting, they'll kill anything or anyone. If only they could see how silly they look — that'd put a stop to their daft antics. What every survival kit needs — a mirror...

Simon finds the dead airman

1) Simon finds the body of the <u>dead airman</u>. He understands that it's "<u>the beast</u>", and that he needs to <u>tell</u> the others it's "<u>harmless</u>".

2) Piggy <u>senses</u> that <u>trouble</u> is coming. He suggests that they go to Jack's feast "<u>to make sure nothing happens</u>", and later he urges Ralph to <u>leave</u>, saying "<u>There's going to be trouble</u>".

> **Theme — Nature**
>
> Golding creates the sense that something <u>terrible</u> will happen by describing the <u>storm</u> that's developing. The air's "<u>ready to explode</u>" and the clouds "brooded".

Jack's power grows

1) <u>All</u> of the boys go to <u>Jack's feast</u> — even Ralph and Piggy. They're attracted by the promise of <u>meat</u>, and the "partly secure society" of the larger <u>group</u>.

2) Jack wears garlands "like an <u>idol</u>" and is <u>ordering</u> the boys around — he's <u>abusing</u> his power. He promises "<u>food</u>", "<u>fun</u>" and <u>protection</u> "from the beast" to get the boys to join his tribe — he uses their <u>fear</u> to <u>control</u> them.

3) Jack says the conch "<u>doesn't count</u>" at his end of the island. He's <u>rejecting civilisation</u> and the <u>rules</u> of their old life.

© AF archive / Alamy

The tribe murders Simon

KEY EVENT

1) Ralph points out that a <u>storm's</u> coming, and that Jack has <u>no shelters</u> — the boys react "uneasily", showing that they're still <u>drawn to civilisation</u>. Jack distracts them by ordering them to "<u>Dance!</u>"

2) Simon crawls into the <u>centre</u> of the dance. He's described as "a <u>thing</u>" and "the <u>beast</u>" — the tribe is <u>confused</u> and scared by the darkness, the storm, and the <u>savage</u> dance. He's also described as "<u>Simon</u>" — deep down the boys <u>recognise</u> him, but they're <u>too scared</u> and <u>frenzied</u> to stop.

> **Turning point in the action**
>
> The boys' savagery and violence reaches a peak when they murder Simon.

> **Theme — Nature**
>
> The storm reaches a <u>climax</u> during the dance — the air is "<u>dark and terrible</u>", with the "explosion" of <u>lightning</u>. After Simon's death, Golding creates a very <u>peaceful</u> atmosphere to <u>contrast</u> with the frenzied dance and to emphasise Simon's <u>innocent</u> and <u>spiritual</u> nature.

3) The boys act as a "<u>single organism</u>" when they murder Simon — they've lost their <u>individual identities</u>. They kill him without "<u>words</u>", only "<u>the tearing of teeth and claws</u>" — they've become <u>inhuman</u> and their savage instincts have <u>taken over</u>.

KEY QUOTE

"Cut his throat! Spill his blood! Do him in!"

Simon's death is a big turning point in the book. Hints of violence have been there all along (like Roger throwing those stones) but now they've committed full-blown murder. The violence escalates pretty quickly.

Chapter Ten Analysis — The Shell and the Glasses

Sorry if you thought this was going to be a lovely, uplifting book about some jolly adventures on a tropical island. It's more like the Christmas episode of your favourite soap — things keep getting worse and worse...

The boys react to Simon's murder in different ways

1) Ralph is the only character who admits that it was murder. He's still civilised enough to take responsibility for his actions, but he accepts Piggy's excuse that they were "only on the outside".

> **Theme — Evil**
>
> Simon's murder makes Ralph see that there's evil in everyone — even himself.

2) Piggy claims it was just an accident caused by the dance and won't take any responsibility — he can't accept that the savagery and evil he sees in Jack is also in himself and Ralph.

3) Jack tells the tribe that they attacked the beast, but says that it can't be killed. He also says the beast was disguised — this suggests that the tribe might have to attack someone else if Jack tells them it's the beast. It's also a way for them to avoid feeling guilty about it.

Ralph has lost all his power to Jack

1) Only Ralph, Piggy, Sam and Eric are left to look after the littluns and keep the fire going. Piggy insists that Ralph's "still Chief", but Ralph realises that Jack has all the power.

2) Ralph is "cradling" the conch and holding it "caressingly" — he's trying to get some comfort from this symbol of civilisation. It's useless now — the rules of civilisation mean nothing.

> **Theme — Power and Leadership**
>
> Jack is "going to beat Wilfred" for no reason — this senseless violence stops the boys from challenging his authority.

© Moviestore collection Ltd / Alamy

Jack's tribe steal Piggy's glasses

1) Jack attacks Ralph's group in the night and takes Piggy's glasses so his tribe can make fire. It's the first act of planned violence towards other humans. It foreshadows Piggy's murder in the next chapter.

> Ralph is surprised that they didn't take the conch. He hasn't realised that the conch — and all it stands for — is of no interest to Jack.

> **Theme — Civilisation and Barbarity**
>
> Ralph gradually forgets what the fire is for. This shows that he's losing his grip on civilised values.

2) The signal fire represents the boys' hope of being rescued. The fire has died, and there isn't any way of relighting it without Piggy's glasses. This symbolises the death of hope in Ralph's group.

EXAM TIP

Show how Jack controls the other boys...

Jack doesn't use his power for good. He beats Wilfred for no reason and says that the beast can assume any disguise, which means it could return and attack again — you can say he uses the boys' fear to control them.

Chapter Eleven Analysis — Castle Rock

You'd think they'd all come to their senses after killing Simon, but things just go from bad to worse. Ralph's only got three supporters and the conch left, and something tells me Jack doesn't much care about the conch...

Ralph and Piggy still believe in the power of the conch

1) Ralph's group still use the conch to take it in turns to speak — they're clinging to democracy and the old rules.

2) Piggy believes that if he goes to Jack holding the conch, Jack will return his glasses because "right's right". He still believes the conch can inspire decent behaviour.

3) Ralph blows the conch at Castle Rock but the tribe doesn't respond — the conch has lost its authority, as has Ralph.

© AF archive / Alamy

The atmosphere at Castle Rock is hostile

1) Golding doesn't name many of the boys in the tribe — most of them are just "savages".

2) At first, the savages are just trying to "defend the entrance" to Castle Rock. They get more and more aggressive towards Ralph's group, eventually becoming "a solid mass of menace".

Language

By the end of this chapter, Golding stops using Jack's name — instead he writes "the Chief". He's completely lost his old identity as Jack Merridew, choirboy, and is now the nameless Chief of a tribe of nameless "savages".

3) The fight between Ralph and Jack represents the open conflict between civilisation and savagery. Ralph still believes he can make Jack see reason — he doesn't see that Jack is no longer held back by morals.

Piggy's death symbolises the death of logic and reason

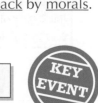

1) Piggy points out to the tribe how savage they've become. The boys are angry, but Roger is calm and he deliberately levers a rock off the cliff onto Piggy. It kills Piggy and destroys the conch, the symbol of civilisation and Ralph's democratic leadership.

Theme — Evil

Roger kills Piggy with "delirious abandonment" — he's turned into a cold-blooded killer. At the end of the chapter it's clear that he's become a torturer too.

2) The tribe "jeer" and shriek but as soon as they realise Piggy is dead, there's complete silence — this shows how shocked they are.

3) Simon was killed in a frenzy of fear, but Piggy's murder is deliberate — Jack declares "I meant that!" Jack and Roger are so savage that they feel no guilt about the murder.

4) Jack tries to kill Ralph, but he escapes through "instinct". He's now a hunted animal, not a civilised human.

Make sure you understand the important symbols...

This chapter's packed with symbolism — in the exam, don't forget to explain what the symbols mean. For example, the conch breaking into "a thousand white fragments" symbolises the ultimate end of democracy.

Chapter Twelve Analysis — Cry of the Hunters

This is it. The final chapter. Things aren't looking good for Ralph — Piggy's dead, Jack wants to kill him and he's still trapped on an island in the middle of the Pacific Ocean. It couldn't possibly get any worse... could it?

Ralph realises that his life is in danger

1) Ralph tries to <u>convince</u> himself that Piggy's death was an "<u>accident</u>", but he <u>knows</u> that Jack will "<u>never let him alone</u>".

2) Sam and Eric tell him that Roger has "<u>sharpened a stick at both ends</u>" — this doesn't make sense to Ralph, but it suggests to the reader that the tribe plans to put <u>Ralph's</u> head on a stick, <u>like the pig</u>.

3) The tribe <u>lights a fire</u> to smoke Ralph out. It sounds like a "<u>drum-roll</u>" — the same sound as the fire that <u>killed</u> the <u>littlun</u>. It hints that <u>someone</u> might <u>die</u> in this fire, too.

> **Symbolism**
>
> Ralph, the most <u>civilised</u> character, destroys the Lord of the Flies — the symbol of <u>evil</u> and <u>barbarity</u>. In Chapter Eleven Roger, the least <u>civilised</u> character, destroyed the conch — the symbol of <u>civilisation</u> and <u>order</u>.

Golding's language creates a terrifying atmosphere

1) Golding describes the hunt from Ralph's <u>point of view</u> to emphasise how scared Ralph is.

2) He uses <u>short sentences</u>, and lots of <u>punctuation</u>, e.g. "Hide, break the line, climb a tree — which was the best after all?" This <u>speeds up</u> the action and gives a sense of the <u>panic</u> Ralph's feeling.

3) Ralph is "screaming, snarling, bloody". Golding uses <u>animal imagery</u> to <u>link</u> Ralph to the hunted pigs.

Ralph is saved by a naval officer

> **Turning point in the action**
> Ralph's saved just as his death seems certain.

1) Ralph and the savages run into a <u>naval officer</u> on the beach. <u>Ironically</u>, the fire that was meant to <u>smoke out</u> Ralph has <u>attracted a ship</u>. At their most <u>barbaric</u>, the boys have made sure they'll return to <u>civilisation</u>.

© 1999 Topham Picturepoint

2) The officer <u>imagines</u> that it's been like an <u>adventure story</u>. He's shocked when Ralph tells him <u>two boys</u> have been <u>killed</u>. Golding is <u>reminding</u> the reader that classic adventure stories present <u>human nature</u> in an <u>unrealistically optimistic</u> way.

3) Ralph bursts into <u>tears</u> — he's been <u>rescued</u>, but he's lost his <u>innocence</u>. He realises that there is <u>evil in everyone</u> and it's only held back by society's <u>rules</u>.

4) Neither <u>civilisation</u> nor <u>barbarity</u> wins at the end of the novel. The savages don't <u>kill Ralph</u> — who represents <u>civilisation</u>. But the boys go back to a <u>world at war</u> understanding the nature of man's evil.

> **Theme — Civilisation and Barbarity**
>
> The officer's <u>gun</u> and the <u>warship</u> are <u>reminders</u> that there's a <u>savage war</u> going on in the outside, <u>grown-up</u> world.

"Ralph wept for the end of innocence"

Ralph has seen the true nature of mankind and has witnessed two blameless characters being killed by savage mobs. Things could be worse though — he could be stuck revising for his GCSE English exam...

Practice Questions

So you've now been through the whole of Section One. And what a section it was. Anyway, enough of this waffle — it's time to see how much you remember. You only need to write a few words to answer each quick question, but you'll need to write about a paragraph for each of the lovely in-depth ones...

Quick Questions

1) What does Ralph use to gather everyone together in Chapter One?
   a) a megaphone
   b) a conch shell
   c) a trumpet

2) Why does the passing ship not see the signal fire in Chapter Four?

3) How is Ralph and Simon's last shelter different from the first one that all the boys built?

4) What does Simon discover when he goes to see the beast in Chapter Nine?

5) What happens to Ralph in the end?

In-depth Questions

1) The littlun with the birthmark dies in the fire in Chapter Two.
   Suggest reasons why this event is significant.

2) Compare how Jack and Ralph deal with the boys' fears in Chapter Five.

3) Do you agree with Simon's theory that the beast is the boys themselves? Why?

4) When Jack fails to remove Ralph as chief he declares himself chief of his own tribe.
   Why do you think some of the boys follow him?

5) Why does Piggy decide to take the conch with him when he goes to ask Jack's tribe
   for his glasses in Chapter Eleven?

Practice Questions

If you've whizzed through the warm-up questions, it's time for some slightly scarier ones. These will help you think about the book in more depth — and also give you a bit of practice for your exam. You don't need to write a full essay for all of them — just writing a plan can be helpful.

Exam-style Questions

1) 'It is clear from the start of *Lord of the Flies* that things are going to go badly for the characters.' How far do you agree with this statement?

2) Read the passage where Jack returns from his first kill in Chapter Four, from "Ralph spoke. 'You let the fire out…'" to "Piggy cried out in terror: 'My specs!'" How does Golding make this such a powerful moment in the novel?

3) How is the character of Piggy essential to the plot of *Lord of the Flies*?

4) How does Golding present the changing relationship between Ralph and Jack?

5) At the end of the novel Ralph weeps for the "end of innocence". How does Golding express ideas about the loss of innocence in *Lord of the Flies*?

Character Profile — Ralph

Ralph is the main character in *Lord of the Flies*. Golding has packed him full of admirable qualities, so it's easy for the reader to like him. Although you wouldn't want to be Ralph, not with friends like his...

Ralph represents the theme of civilisation

1) Ralph is <u>built</u> a bit like "<u>a boxer</u>". This makes him seem <u>powerful</u>. There's a "<u>mildness</u> about his mouth" that suggests he's <u>kind</u> and <u>good-natured</u>.

2) He has a strong sense of <u>fair play</u>. He's <u>shocked</u> when Jack punches Piggy and snatches his glasses.

3) He's <u>brave</u>, even though he doesn't always feel it — e.g. he makes himself <u>go first</u> to Castle Rock. He also has a strong sense of <u>responsibility</u> — e.g. he makes sure Piggy will <u>look after</u> the littluns when he goes looking for the beast.

> **Theme — Civilisation and Barbarity**
>
> • Ralph represents <u>law and order</u>. He <u>takes charge</u> of the boys and gives them jobs to make the island a <u>better</u> place to live. He says they'll use the <u>conch</u> to <u>take it in turns</u> to speak.
>
> • Ralph clings to the hope of <u>rescue</u> and returning to <u>civilisation</u>.

© Moviestore collection Ltd / Alamy

> **Ralph is...**
>
> **Determined:** "I'm chief. I'll go. Don't argue."
>
> **Brave:** "Ralph picked up his stick and prepared for battle."
>
> **Fair:** "The choir belongs to you, of course."
>
> **Honest:** "We'd talk but we wouldn't fight a tiger. We'd hide."

He isn't always perfect

1) He gets involved in <u>laughing</u> at Piggy or Simon in a way that shows he's capable of <u>hurting others</u>.

2) He sometimes <u>gives in</u> to his <u>instincts</u> — he <u>gnaws</u> at his meat "like a wolf" and gets <u>excited</u> when he <u>wounds</u> a pig.

3) He <u>takes part</u> in the dance when Simon is <u>killed</u>. Later he's <u>ashamed</u> of it, but he lets Piggy persuade him that it wasn't their fault. This is a sign that <u>even Ralph</u> is slipping into <u>savagery</u>.

> **Theme — Evil**
>
> By involving Ralph, the <u>hero</u>, in acts of <u>evil</u>, Golding shows that there is evil in <u>everyone</u>.

He can't always think straight

1) He tries to plan an important assembly <u>speech</u> but he finds himself lost in a "<u>maze of thoughts</u>" that he can't quite put into words. He realises that he can't <u>think</u> as well as <u>Piggy</u> can.

2) He wants things to be <u>straightforward</u>. He says they should <u>talk</u> about the beast and "decide there's nothing in it". He's <u>annoyed</u> that he can't make the <u>other</u> boys see his point of view.

> This is a reminder that <u>all</u> the characters in *Lord of the Flies* are <u>children</u>. They can't solve their problems using reason and logic. This <u>foreshadows</u> later events and builds an <u>atmosphere</u> of <u>fear</u>.

Character Profile — Ralph

Ralph's pretty important. Not only is he the elected chief of a small group of schoolboys running around with pointy sticks, it turns out he also represents the struggle of all mankind against evil and barbarity... Intense.

Ralph's relationship with Piggy changes

1) At first, Ralph gets irritated by Piggy's questions and is scornful of his clumsiness and asthma. He thinks that Piggy's "matter-of-fact ideas were dull", but he enjoys teasing him.

2) By the time he holds an assembly about the beast, Ralph has realised that Piggy is a good thinker. He relies more and more on Piggy's sense and intelligence.

3) When he is being hunted, he realises how much he needs Piggy to "talk sense".

> Ralph's relationship with Piggy shows that he's willing to change his opinions. Golding uses this to show how Ralph develops as a character.

His relationship with Jack is complicated

1) At first, it looks like Ralph and Jack could be friends. They smile at each other with "shy liking".

2) They fall out when Jack and his hunters are too busy hunting and having fun to build the shelters and keep the fire going. This is the first sign that they can't resolve the conflict between fun and responsibility.

3) After a disagreement, Ralph asks Jack openly why he hates him. Ralph realises that Jack needs to lead.

> **Theme — Civilisation and Barbarity**
> Golding uses the conflict between Ralph and Jack to represent the conflict between civilisation and barbarity on the island.

> Ralph and Jack's rocky relationship creates a feeling of tension for the reader — only one of them can win.

4) Ralph sees that there is an "indefinable connection" between him and Jack which means Jack can't leave him alone. Jack's got something to prove.

His emotions change

Ralph's emotions show the story changing from one of exciting adventure, into one of terrifying violence:

1) At first, Ralph is delighted with the island. He's excited that there are no grown-ups and expects to have fun. He's also confident that adults will rescue them — he trusts the civilised world.

2) Later on, he feels the "wearisomeness" of life on the island. It's not the adventure he expected. He begins to feel insecure. His old "understandable and lawful world" begins to slip away.

3) His deepest despair comes right at the end of the book. The boys are rescued — but Ralph realises that his innocent view of a fair and decent world is lost forever.

> **Theme — Evil**
> Ralph realises that evil exists inside everyone. He recognises it in himself but fights it — this represents man's struggle against evil.

KEY QUOTE

"The tears began to flow and sobs shook him."

Things start well for Ralph, but by the end, all of his friends have been killed or deserted him, he's realised that all humans are evil, and he's being hunted down by a nasty mob wielding pointy sticks... Bad times.

Character Profile — Piggy

Poor Piggy has a bit of a rough deal in the novel. He's nice and is really quite clever, but because he looks different, he gets picked on and has his ideas ignored. And then he gets killed. Poor Piggy.

Piggy is an outsider

1) Piggy's <u>appearance</u> makes him <u>comical</u> to the other boys. He's <u>fat</u>, <u>clumsy</u>, has <u>asthma</u> and wears <u>glasses</u>. He's also not as <u>well-spoken</u> as the others, and doesn't really have a <u>sense of humour</u>. The reader never finds out Piggy's <u>real name</u> — he's <u>defined</u> by his appearance.

© AF archive / Alamy

2) Piggy's very vulnerable to <u>bullying</u>. Jack <u>breaks</u> Piggy's glasses and <u>mimics</u> him — even Ralph can't help <u>smiling</u> about it.

3) The others don't take him <u>seriously</u>. They tell him to <u>shut up</u> when he has ideas, but they pay attention to the <u>same ideas</u> from other people.

Theme — Civilisation and Barbarity

As the boys become <u>more savage</u>, they find it <u>easier</u> to kill the pigs. This <u>symbolises</u> the boys' <u>rejection</u> of civilisation — the thing Piggy <u>values most</u>. By the time they kill <u>Piggy</u>, they're <u>completely savage</u>.

Piggy is...

Intelligent: "what intelligence had been shown was traceable to Piggy".

Logical: "The first thing we ought to have made was shelters".

Loyal: "the true, wise friend called Piggy".

Piggy cares about proper behaviour

1) Piggy's always reminding the others that the <u>conch</u> gives him the <u>right to speak</u>. He reminds them that Ralph is the <u>chief</u> and that they should <u>obey</u> him.

2) He tells Jack he should give him his <u>glasses</u> back because it's the <u>right</u> thing to do. This shows that he can be <u>brave</u>.

3) He wonders what <u>grown-ups</u> would say. He longs for the <u>order</u> and <u>structure</u> that adults impose.

Theme — Civilisation and Barbarity

Piggy tries to maintain <u>rules</u> and to impose the <u>civilised society</u> he craves on the other boys. Piggy and the <u>conch</u> are destroyed <u>together</u>, symbolising the <u>end</u> of <u>civilisation</u> on the island.

He often acts like an adult

1) He says the boys are like a "crowd of <u>kids</u>" when they go rushing off to light a fire. He goes after them with the "martyred expression of a <u>parent</u>".

Theme — Games

Piggy never <u>joins in</u> with other boys' games. Golding keeps him <u>separate</u>, which makes it even more <u>shocking</u> when he's involved in Simon's <u>murder</u>.

Theme — Nature

Piggy is less <u>in tune</u> with nature than the others — this is <u>symbolised</u> by the way his <u>hair</u> doesn't <u>grow</u>.

2) When the <u>fire</u> gets out of control, he points out that it has destroyed their stock of <u>firewood</u> and could ruin the <u>fruit</u> they need.

3) There are times when Ralph <u>despairs</u> about what will happen. That's when Piggy says they just have to <u>carry on</u> because that's what "<u>grown-ups</u> would do".

Character Profile — Piggy

Piggy only ever tried to be good, sensible and kind. The others think he's annoying because he often sounds like a grown-up, but it seems a bit harsh to do away with him in a nasty head-splitting boulder incident...

He's kind to the littluns

Theme — Fear

Piggy tries to deal with the littluns' fear of the beast logically. He gets frustrated when they won't listen to reason.

1) Piggy helps the littlun with the birthmark to speak in the assembly, repeating his whispered words aloud.

2) He feels confident with the littluns because they're smaller and younger than him.

He's loyal and supportive to Ralph

1) He's not sure about Ralph at first, only voting for him as chief "grudgingly". But once he gets to know him, he sticks by him. He speaks up for Ralph when the others interrupt him.

Theme — Power and Leadership

Piggy doesn't have any leadership qualities himself, but he sees them in Ralph — he stays loyal to him when all the others have joined Jack's tribe.

2) He offers advice — e.g. he senses that there's going to be trouble on the night that Simon dies and advises Ralph to "Come away".

3) He whispers reminders and encouragement when Ralph forgets his important ideas. He keeps his faith in Ralph as a good chief right up to the end.

Piggy represents the logical side of civilisation

Theme — Civilisation and Barbarity

Piggy's logic stops him from seeing how far from civilisation the others have slipped, e.g. he still trusts the power of the conch to make others respect him at Castle Rock.

1) Piggy's a thinker — he starts to work out ways of making the fire smoke more, and he even suggests making a sundial.

2) After Jack goes, Piggy suggests that they light a fire on the beach. He feels proud when the others actually do it.

3) He has important insights about people too:

- He sees that Jack is full of hatred and knows that he could hurt people.

- He doesn't think anyone should be frightened on the island, unless they are "frightened of people". He's exactly right.

- He realises that the boys are losing their hold on normal behaviour. He joins in with Simon's murder, which shows that even he is giving in to fear and savagery.

KEY QUOTE

"I tell you, I got the conch!"

Piggy stands for logic. This is made clear in the way he believes in the power of the conch — he's trying to get order back into their lives. What with all the spearing and creepy face painting, who can blame him?

Character Profile — Jack

Jack's power-hungry — he loves the feeling of being in charge. You can tell it from his very first appearance on the beach. But he's not a good, kind leader — he enjoys punishing people. Nasty.

Jack wants to be in control

© Photos 12 / Alamy

1) Jack is "ugly without silliness" and his eyes are "turning, or ready to turn, to anger". This suggests he can be bad-tempered and nasty.

2) Jack bosses the choir around, but they don't actually like him. They vote for him to be chief with "dreary obedience".

3) Out of all the boys, "the most obvious leader was Jack" and Jack himself claims that he "ought to be chief".

4) He hates Ralph being in charge and often challenges him. He says Ralph can't hunt to provide meat, so he has no right to tell them what to do.

5) He makes up rules to suit himself, such as saying that the conch "doesn't count" at his end of the island. He rejects the rules when they don't suit him, shouting "Bollocks to the rules!"

Theme — Civilisation and Barbarity

Jack doesn't see the value in building shelters or keeping the fire going. He's rejecting civilisation.

Theme — Fear

Jack uses the other characters' fear to control them, e.g. he says "my hunters will protect you from the beast" to get people to join his tribe.

Jack is...

Arrogant: "I ought to be chief".

Proud: "the freckles on Jack's face disappeared under a blush of mortification".

Violent: "I cut the pig's throat".

Controlling: "What d'you mean by not joining my tribe?"

He prefers fun to responsibility

1) Jack only wants to enjoy himself on the island. He's the first character to forget about the possibility of rescue.

2) Jack represents the point of view that says people should do whatever they want to, regardless of morals or logic.

3) Jack thinks he'd be a good leader, but he doesn't look after the weaker boys as a leader should:

- He bullies Piggy.
- He calls the littluns "cry-babies" for being afraid of the beast.
- He doesn't sort out shelters for his tribe.

Theme — Power and Leadership

The conflict between Jack and Ralph is between two different types of leadership. Ralph is voted in and tries to do what's best for the group — get them rescued. Jack takes power for himself and just wants to have a good time.

Character Profile — Jack

Jack's a bit immature in my opinion. He just wants it his way and can't handle not getting it. I think I'd rather be stuck on an island with almost any of the other characters instead of Jack. Except maybe Roger...

He's naturally violent and aggressive

1) Jack's <u>vicious</u> with his <u>words</u>, especially to <u>Piggy</u>. He calls him "<u>Fatty</u>" to make the others laugh and tells him to "<u>Shut up</u>". Later, he <u>punches</u> Piggy and <u>smacks</u> him in the head when Piggy <u>criticises</u> him.

Language

Jack's <u>aggressive</u> way of speaking <u>foreshadows</u> his violent behaviour later on in the novel.

Theme — Evil

Jack becomes <u>more evil</u> as the story goes on. He <u>represents</u> the <u>evil</u> that Golding believed was in <u>everyone</u>, and that would <u>come out</u> if the <u>rules of society</u> were taken away.

2) When he has his <u>own</u> tribe, Jack gives up <u>pretending</u> to be fair, and <u>rules</u> as a <u>dictator</u>. He uses violence to keep control of his tribe, e.g. Wilfred is <u>tied up</u> and <u>beaten</u> for no reason.

3) After Piggy's <u>death</u>, Jack hurls his spear straight at Ralph. His <u>violence</u> is open and <u>deliberate</u>.

He has a strong sense of pride

Jack's <u>pride</u> makes him <u>cruel</u>. He treats his tribe like <u>servants</u>, e.g. making them say "The <u>Chief</u> has spoken". He doesn't see them as <u>human beings</u> — this might explain why he's able to <u>hurt</u> them so <u>easily</u>.

1) Losing the vote for chief to Ralph damages Jack's <u>pride</u>. This sets him <u>against</u> Ralph from the beginning of the story.

2) He <u>challenges</u> Ralph's <u>authority</u>, and gets angry if he's <u>criticised</u>.

3) He makes a big deal of not being a <u>coward</u>. He's always <u>teasing</u> people for being <u>afraid</u>, and he can't bear Ralph's suggestion that <u>he's</u> afraid to go and find the beast.

He becomes more and more obsessed with hunting

1) Jack always <u>goes further</u> than any of the other boys — he's the <u>first</u> to <u>injure</u> a pig and the first to <u>kill</u> one.

2) He starts to have a "<u>compulsion</u> to track down and <u>kill</u>". A "<u>madness</u>" comes into his eyes when he thinks of <u>hunting</u>. This is an <u>early</u> sign of his <u>savagery</u>, which grows throughout the novel.

© Moviestore collection Ltd / Alamy

Theme — Civilisation and Barbarity

Jack's <u>growing obsession</u> with hunting represents how the group <u>lose</u> their sense of <u>civilisation</u>, and become more <u>barbaric</u>.

3) Golding makes Jack <u>sound</u> like an <u>animal</u>, describing his "<u>bloodthirsty snarling</u>". Once he <u>paints</u> his face he doesn't see <u>himself</u> any more, he sees an "<u>awesome stranger</u>". This allows him not to feel <u>responsible</u> for his actions.

Write about how characters change in the novel...

Jack becomes more and more savage as the story progresses — but at the end of the novel he becomes a "little boy" again. Make sure you know how each character develops and what Golding is trying to show.

Character Profile — Simon

Simon's a funny one — a quiet sort, but an interesting character. He's the kind of guy who hovers around in the background being helpful and kind, but who wouldn't necessarily get invited to lots of exciting parties.

Simon is shy and physically weak

> **Simon is...**
>
> **Kind:** "Simon found for them the fruit they could not reach".
>
> **Perceptive:** "maybe there is a beast... maybe it's only us."
>
> **Solitary:** "He... glanced swiftly round to confirm that he was utterly alone".

Courtesy of MGM Media Licensing

1) He's not as <u>old</u> or as <u>tall</u> as the big boys. He's a "<u>skinny, vivid</u>" boy, who sometimes faints. This suggests he's physically <u>weaker</u> than the others, but that there's <u>something</u> quite <u>intense</u> about him.

2) Simon often finds it hard to express himself. He thinks he should try to <u>explain</u> how he feels about the beast, but he hates <u>speaking aloud</u> in front of the others.

> **Theme — Evil**
>
> Simon <u>represents</u> the <u>goodness</u> inside all humans. His <u>weakness</u> shows that, although we <u>all</u> have good in us, the <u>evil</u> is <u>stronger</u>.

3) His failure to <u>explain</u> himself <u>reminds</u> the reader that he's a <u>young</u> boy struggling to express a <u>complicated</u> idea. The others <u>laugh</u> at him, and Piggy says he's "<u>cracked</u>" — their attitude towards him <u>hints</u> that they won't accept that the beast is <u>inside them</u> in time to control it.

Simon is kind and perceptive

1) Simon seems to <u>know</u> how to <u>help</u> — he <u>senses</u> Ralph's despair and <u>comforts</u> him, telling him that he'll "<u>get back all right</u>". Ralph tells him he's "<u>batty</u>", but Simon's <u>prediction</u> turns out to be <u>right</u>.

2) When Jack knocks Piggy's <u>glasses</u> off, Simon <u>hands</u> them back. Jack won't give Piggy <u>meat</u>, but Simon gives Piggy <u>his own</u>.

3) He's very <u>sensitive</u> to all the <u>hostility</u> and emotion amongst the boys when arguments break out. He feels surrounded by passions which "<u>beat about</u>" him with "<u>awful wings</u>".

> **Theme — Evil**
>
> Simon's comment, "<u>As if it wasn't a good island</u>" gives the reader a clue that this story isn't going to be a normal <u>adventure</u> story, and that there is <u>evil</u> on the island.

> **Theme — Fear**
>
> Simon recognises that the <u>real</u> thing to fear is <u>themselves</u>. The other boys <u>savagely kill</u> him when he tries to <u>tell</u> them this. This is <u>ironic</u> — their <u>fear</u> of the beast causes them to kill the person who could tell them that the beast <u>isn't real</u>.

4) He doesn't believe in the <u>beast</u> as a real <u>creature</u> that lives in the forest. When he thinks of the <u>beast</u>, he thinks of <u>humans</u>. He tries to <u>explain</u> this to the others but they <u>don't understand</u>.

5) Simon's conversation with the <u>Lord of the Flies</u> happens in his <u>head</u>. It tells him what he <u>already knows</u> — that the <u>evil</u> the boys fear is in <u>themselves</u>. He goes <u>back</u> to tell the others, wanting to <u>reassure</u> them, but it leads to his <u>death</u>.

Character Profile — Simon

Simon's a really nice boy, and he works out that the beast is just the boys' inner evil while the others are still running around screaming. If only he hadn't been brutally murdered, how different things might have been...

He's quite a spiritual figure

1) Some people think Simon represents a figure like Jesus. He never does anything to harm people, he hands out food to the littluns and makes a prediction about the future. He dies because he tries to tell the others the truth and they reject it. But unlike the death of Jesus, Simon's death only leads to more savagery, not to the boys' salvation.

Theme — Civilisation and Barbarity

Ralph represents civilisation and Jack represents savagery but Simon's separate — he doesn't seem to be affected by the pull of barbarity.

Theme — Evil

Simon's secret part of the forest is beautiful and calm until the hunters leave the pig's head there. This symbolises the way evil destroys innocence.

2) The descriptions of Simon sometimes sound religious. His body seems to turn to silver and "marble" as it's washed out to sea, as if it's something heavenly. The water surrounds his head with "brightness" like an angel's halo.

3) After Simon's death, the weather becomes very calm and the sea gently takes his body away — it's as if nature is mourning Simon's death. This is an example of pathetic fallacy — Golding describes nature as if it has human feelings.

4) Simon's secret place in the forest is full of "candle buds" which open wide as he sits alone at dusk. It makes you think of candles in a peaceful church. It is spiritual and calm.

© iStockphoto.com / SZE FEI WONG

Theme — Evil

The conversation between Simon and the Lord of the Flies is a confrontation between good and evil.

Simon's murder changes everything

1) Simon's death is horrific. The boys use their bare hands and their teeth to beat and tear at Simon. It is animal-like savagery which even involves Piggy and Ralph.

Theme — Civilisation and Barbarity

Simon's murder is the point of no return. The boys can't go back to being civilised.

Theme — Evil

The boys' evil has progressed from killing a pig for food, to laughing as they kill one, and then to murder.

2) Simon's death shows you what even the most decent human beings are capable of. It's the beginning of open savagery.

EXAM TIP

Make sure you know what each character symbolises...

Simon, Jack, Piggy and Ralph represent different things. Simon stands for natural goodness that no-one else in the novel seems to have — they all struggle with inner evil whereas Simon has inner goodness.

Character Profile — Roger

Roger's a really nasty piece of work. He always seems to pop up when anything really horrible is happening in the story. I didn't like him as soon he kicked over those sand castles. I like sand castles...

Roger's a bully

1) Roger is "slight" and "furtive" and has an "inner intensity". This makes him sound secretive and threatening.

Roger is...

Merciless: "Roger sharpened a stick at both ends."

Cruel: "You don't know Roger. He's a terror."

© Moviestore collection Ltd / Alamy

2) Roger suggests having a vote for chief, but he supports Jack when he tries to take over the island. He's the first to call Jack "Chief".

3) Golding describes a "darker shadow" crossing Roger's face when Jack calls him over — this suggests there could be rivalry between them.

Theme — Power and Leadership

Jack gets his power from violence, which is often carried out by Roger.

Roger's involved in most of the important action

1) Roger doesn't say much, but he's around during a lot of the main events of the novel — particularly the violent ones.

Theme — Civilisation and Barbarity

Roger becomes more savage than any of the other characters — he shows just how far it's possible to get from civilisation.

2) Roger's power increases as Jack begins to take control of the island. Jack creates a violent, brutal dictatorship. Roger is the sort of person who fits in well with that.

He gets more and more vicious

1) His first experiments with violence are when he throws stones around Henry on the beach. He throws "to miss" — "the taboo of the old life" stops him from hurting Henry, but this is a hint of what he's capable of.

Theme — Evil

By the end of the novel, Roger's evil, savage side has taken over completely.

2) When hunting, Roger sticks his spear up the mother sow's backside — it's cruel and unnecessary.

3) He starts off throwing small stones at Piggy at Castle Rock, then levers the boulder onto Piggy and kills him.

4) He takes on the role of torturer to force Sam and Eric to join Jack's tribe. He has to almost push Jack out of the way to do it — it's another hint of the rivalry between them.

5) He sharpens a stick at both ends to hunt Ralph with. It suggests that he's thinking of sticking Ralph's head on it as they did with the pig — a horrific idea.

EXAM TIP

Create your own notes on each character...

Look back through the novel for references to Roger and learn some quotes too. Do this for each character, then when you get into the exam, you'll be prepared for whatever they throw at you. Hopefully not spears.

Character Profile — The Littluns

The littluns don't get very much air-time in the book, because most of the older boys just ignore them. Don't make the same mistake — they have important effects on the plot and the themes of the novel.

The Littluns live in a little world of their own

1) The littluns automatically <u>obey</u> Ralph because he behaves like an <u>adult</u>. They'll follow anyone who provides for their <u>basic needs</u>.

2) They spend their days <u>playing</u>. Henry is so absorbed in his <u>games</u> on the sand that he doesn't notice Roger <u>stalking</u> him. It shows the reader how <u>vulnerable</u> they are.

Theme — Power and Leadership
Ralph takes on the <u>responsibility</u> of <u>looking after</u> the littluns, but Jack <u>doesn't care</u> about them.

Theme — Games
The littluns <u>join in</u> with the tribe's <u>hunting dance</u> — their <u>games</u> have become much less <u>innocent</u>.

3) They're difficult to <u>organise</u>. They "<u>scattered</u> everywhere" when Piggy tried to take their <u>names</u>.

They quickly lose their civilised values

1) When Piggy asks <u>Percival</u> for his name at the <u>beginning</u> of the story, he <u>recites</u> his full name and <u>address</u>. By the end of the book, his <u>whole identity</u> has "<u>faded clean away</u>", even his <u>name</u>. This shows how much of their <u>old lives</u> the boys have <u>forgotten</u>.

Theme — Civilisation and Barbarity
Percival forgetting his <u>name</u> is a clear sign that the boys have moved from <u>civilisation</u> to <u>barbarity</u>.

2) The littluns don't help with <u>building</u> the shelters and they go to the <u>toilet</u> all over the place. Ralph loses his <u>temper</u> with them because he feels they're <u>slipping</u> away from <u>civilised</u> values.

© AF archive / Alamy

Some people think that the <u>littluns</u> represent the <u>general public</u>. They don't <u>think for themselves</u>, they just <u>follow</u> the strongest <u>leader</u> — first <u>Ralph</u>, then <u>Jack</u>.

The littluns represent the theme of fear

Theme — Fear
It's the littluns' <u>fears</u> that bring the <u>idea</u> of the <u>beast</u> to life. It starts off as a <u>nightmare</u>, but more and more boys start to <u>believe</u> that it's real.

1) A littlun is the first one to mention any sort of <u>beast</u>. He talks about a "<u>snake-thing</u>" which turns into <u>creepers</u> in the daylight. It makes the others <u>uneasy</u>.

2) The <u>death</u> of the littlun with the <u>birthmark</u> in the <u>fire</u> is the first <u>clue</u> that this story won't be like a <u>normal adventure</u> story — it's <u>darker</u>, <u>scarier</u> and more real.

"Snakes! Snakes! Look at the snakes!"

The littluns' "beastie" eventually causes the savagery and evil in the boys to emerge. Well done kids. Although I can't help but think that things would've gone downhill anyway, beast or no beast.

Character Profile — The Other Characters

There aren't a huge number of other characters in *Lord of the Flies* (they are stuck on a tropical island, after all), but some of the ones that Golding mentions are important to the themes of the novel.

Sam and Eric are identical twins

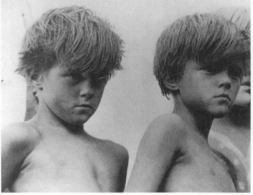

© Photos 12 / Alamy

1) Sam and Eric are <u>cheerful</u>, <u>good-natured</u> and <u>loyal</u> to Ralph when most of the <u>other</u> boys have joined <u>Jack's</u> tribe.

2) They see the <u>dead airman</u> before anyone else. They <u>exaggerate</u> what they saw, which <u>convinces</u> everyone that the beast is <u>real</u>.

3) Joining Jack's tribe is "<u>shameful</u>" for Sam and Eric. They try to explain to Ralph that Jack and Roger <u>forced</u> them to join. They give Ralph <u>food and warnings</u>, but <u>give away</u> his hiding place when they're <u>tortured</u>.

> **Theme — Fear**
>
> The <u>twins</u> are an example of how <u>fear</u> can turn even <u>ordinary</u>, very <u>decent</u> people into <u>savages</u>.

Maurice and Robert represent the boys' descent into savagery

1) <u>Maurice</u> is another of Jack's <u>henchmen</u>. He's <u>not</u> as nasty as Jack and Roger. He <u>destroys</u> the littluns' sand castles with Roger but then <u>hurries away</u> because he feels <u>guilty</u>.

> Maurice <u>feels bad</u> because he "still felt the <u>unease</u> of wrong-doing". At this point, he still <u>remembers</u> enough about his <u>old life</u> to know he's done something <u>wrong</u>.

2) <u>Robert</u> acts the part of the <u>pig</u> in a hunting dance and gets slightly <u>hurt</u>. It <u>hints</u> at the <u>danger</u> to come.

> Robert's slight <u>injury</u> shows that the <u>dances</u> are getting more <u>savage</u>. The boys are less able to <u>control themselves</u>.

3) By the end of the story, the <u>tribe</u> all have their <u>faces painted</u> and are simply called "<u>savages</u>". Their names and identities are <u>not important</u> any more as they all behave in the same <u>primitive</u> way.

There are only two adults — and one of them is dead

1) The <u>airman</u> has <u>died</u> in <u>battle</u> and his body lands just after the boys wish for a <u>sign</u> from the <u>grown-up</u> world. It's a <u>disturbing</u> sign — the adults are <u>fighting</u> each other and can't offer the boys <u>safety</u>.

> **Theme — Civilisation and Barbarity**
>
> The officer sees the boys from an <u>outsider's</u> point of view — "<u>little boys</u>". His <u>viewpoint</u> emphasises how <u>savage</u> the boys have become. He has his hand on his <u>revolver</u> — this shows that the <u>outside world</u> is actually just as <u>war-torn</u> and <u>uncivilised</u> as the island.

2) The <u>naval officer</u> who arrives to <u>rescue</u> them is wearing a clean, <u>white uniform</u> which should symbolise <u>order</u> and <u>purity</u>. Ralph has <u>lost</u> his <u>confidence</u> in the adult world though. He knows the uniform only <u>hides</u> the <u>evil</u> that is in all <u>human nature</u>.

EXAM TIP

Don't forget about the minor characters...

They may not say as much as Ralph or Jack, but they're still important — they all add meaning to the book in their own special way. Even that poor dead airman. It's a good idea to include them in your revision.

Practice Questions

Now you've been through the whole section on characters, have a go at these questions to check you've remembered it all. First, here are some quick questions to get you warmed up, and to really get you thinking about who does what, and what all the characters are like.

Quick Questions

1) List three things about Ralph's personality which we might admire.

2) Briefly outline Ralph's changing relationship with Piggy.

3) List four words that describe Piggy.

4) Give an example of one of Piggy's insights into the behaviour or character of others.

5) What would Jack rather do instead of helping to build shelters?

6) Which two of these words describe Jack's character?
   a) arrogant
   b) caring
   c) thoughtful
   d) violent

7) How does Simon feel about speaking in the assembly?

8) What's Roger's first act of violence in the novel?

9) How does a littlun die in Chapter Two?

10) How do Sam and Eric betray Ralph when they're tortured?

Practice Questions

Here are some questions to get you thinking a bit more carefully about the characters in the book — nothing too complicated, just enough to get those brain cells fizzing. Try to write about a paragraph to answer each.

In-depth Questions

1) Why do you think Ralph is chosen as the leader?

2) Who do you think would have been the best leader? Why?

3) Why do you think Ralph calls Piggy "Piggy" in front of the other boys when Piggy has asked him not to?

4) Why do you think the other boys pick on Piggy?

5) Do you think that Simon is a spiritual figure? Why?

6) How does Piggy respond to Simon's death? Suggest reasons for his reaction.

7) Ralph and Jack feel differently about Castle Rock in Chapter Six.
   How do their feelings reflect their personalities?

8) Do you think that Jack has any qualities that make him a good leader?

9) Why do you think Roger is important in Jack's tribe?

10) By the end of the book, Jack's tribe are referred to as "savages" rather than by their names. What does this say about how their personalities have changed?

Practice Questions

Get your pen and paper out — it's time to put your brain in top gear. It's always a good idea to practise answering exam-style questions before you sit your exam, so have a bash at these. You'll need to write longer answers to these, so don't try to answer all of them in one sitting — you'll be there for hours and you might miss your tea.

Exam-style Questions

1) How does Golding make you feel differently about the character of Ralph at the beginning and end of the novel?

2) In Chapter Eight, when Jack tries to take over the tribe, he challenges Ralph to "Call me a coward then".
How does Golding present the character of Jack?

3) Explain which character in *Lord of the Flies* illustrates most clearly the idea that there is both good and evil in everyone.

4) What is the importance of the character of Simon in the novel?

5) Read the passage in Chapter Eight following Jack's departure, from "Piggy was indignant…" to "'between the bathing pool and the platform.'"
How does Golding make you recognise the importance of Simon's and Piggy's thinking in the extract?

Civilisation and Barbarity

Civilisation and the gradual loss of it is pretty much the main theme of *Lord of the Flies*. Even if you just flicked through the book reading random words, you'd notice that most of the boys turn into savages.

At first the boys cling to rules from their old life

1) The boys <u>make rules</u> on the island which are <u>similar</u> to the rules they followed at <u>school</u>. Piggy collects <u>names</u>, just like a school <u>register</u> and they call their meetings "<u>assemblies</u>". They put their <u>hands up</u> to speak, and use the conch to <u>take turns</u>.

> Golding uses the <u>conch</u> as a <u>symbol</u> of <u>civilisation</u> and authority. Its <u>power</u> gradually <u>decreases</u>, which reflects the <u>weakening</u> of <u>civilisation</u> on the island. Its <u>destruction</u> represents the <u>victory</u> of <u>barbarity</u> over civilisation.

Courtesy of Janus Films

2) The <u>rules of home</u> stop them being too <u>violent</u> at first, e.g. Roger doesn't throw stones <u>directly</u> at Henry because of the "<u>taboo of the old life</u>".

The boys react to rules in different ways at first

1) Ralph wants to have <u>fun</u> on the island but he knows that they <u>need rules</u> to make them act <u>responsibly</u>.

2) Jack says they <u>need</u> rules because they're "<u>not savages</u>". It's <u>ironic</u> when you think about how he behaves <u>later on</u> in the book. He also looks forward to <u>punishing</u> anyone who <u>breaks</u> the rules.

3) Piggy is <u>anxious</u> to <u>protect</u> the rules. He gets <u>upset</u> when the other boys don't follow them, calling them "<u>a pack of kids</u>".

Ralph represents civilisation and Jack represents savagery.

Civilised values begin to fade

The boys' increasing <u>violence</u> shows their <u>gradual</u> slip from <u>civilisation</u> to <u>barbarity</u>.

1) The <u>littluns</u> start going to the <u>toilet</u> everywhere, even near their <u>shelters</u>. They quickly <u>forget</u> the <u>civilised</u> values they were taught at <u>home</u>.

2) At first, Jack's <u>hunting</u> fits in with <u>civilised</u> behaviour — he <u>provides meat</u> for all the boys. But the "<u>fierce exhilaration</u>" of hunting soon takes over from <u>sensible behaviour</u>.

3) Jack and the hunters let the <u>fire</u> go out and so <u>miss</u> the chance of <u>rescue</u> — Golding shows that they've <u>forgotten</u> the possibility of <u>returning to civilisation</u> in the savage excitement of hunting.

4) <u>Primitive rituals</u> begin to replace useful <u>rules</u>, e.g. the boys chant, and make an <u>offering</u> to the beast.

5) The "<u>unease</u> of wrong-doing" that stops them hurting each other gradually <u>wears off</u>, and the boys become more <u>violent</u>. The first violent act is when Jack <u>hits</u> Piggy and <u>breaks his glasses</u>.

Piggy's glasses represent reason and logic — breaking them symbolises the break-down of rational thinking.

Civilisation and Barbarity

Ooh look — another page on civilisation and savagery. Anyone would think it was quite an important theme... Have a look back at the handy theme boxes in Sections One and Two as well.

The new society that develops is selfish and violent

1) Jack starts a <u>new group</u> to hunt and "<u>have fun</u>" — he's not interested in <u>rescue</u> or what's <u>best</u> for the group.

2) One of the first things they do is <u>viciously kill</u> a sow.

3) Their basic <u>fears</u> and group <u>instincts</u> control them — they <u>kill Simon</u> in a frenzy. Golding describes the "tearing of teeth and claws" as if the boys are <u>animals</u>.

4) Jack starts handing out <u>violent punishments</u> to enforce his rules — boys are <u>beaten</u> and <u>tortured</u> for no reason.

> This scene is very <u>sexual</u> — Roger sticks his spear "Right up her ass!" and when they kill her they're "heavy and fulfilled" — their <u>emerging sexuality</u> might help explain their <u>violence</u> and <u>savagery</u>.

Appearances change and behaviour becomes more savage

1) The boys' <u>school uniforms</u> represent <u>discipline</u>. They get dirty and torn as the boys <u>lose</u> their old <u>values</u>.

2) Painting his face frees Jack from civilised rules — it provides a "<u>liberation into savagery</u>". The <u>painted faces</u> of the "savages" are like a new <u>uniform</u> — it makes them "anonymous", so no-one has to take individual <u>responsibility</u> for the violence.

> Golding uses the <u>change</u> in the boys' <u>appearances</u> to represent the change in the group from <u>civilisation</u> to <u>savagery</u>.

3) Ralph's group try to "<u>smarten up</u> a bit" to confront Jack's "<u>painted</u>" tribe — they represent <u>civilisation</u> fighting against Jack's <u>barbarity</u>.

4) The <u>officer</u> who rescues them wears a <u>clean white uniform</u>, but the world he represents is <u>at war</u>, just like the boys. Like Ralph, the reader realises that <u>civilised</u> appearances <u>hide</u> the "<u>darkness of man's heart</u>".

The boys follow their natural instincts

1) <u>Nearly all</u> the boys join Jack's <u>tribe</u>, and even <u>Ralph</u> and <u>Piggy</u>, the characters Golding uses to represent <u>civilisation</u>, join in with Simon's <u>murder</u>.

2) Golding is <u>implying</u> that savagery is a more <u>basic</u> human <u>instinct</u> than civilisation. Our urge to behave <u>morally</u> and look after other people is something we're <u>taught</u> by society — <u>not</u> something we're <u>born</u> with.

© AF archive / Alamy

KEY QUOTE

"that understandable and lawful world, was slipping away."

Golding uses a lot of handy symbolism in the novel to show how civilisation is weakening. Basically, anything dirty or broken can symbolise the way the boys have become more savage. It's as easy as that.

Fear

Mention of the beast is one of the first signs that things aren't going to be all sand castles, swimming and coconut milk on the island. First only the littluns get scared. Then everyone does and it all gets a bit silly...

Golding uses the beast to represent the boys' fear

1) The idea that there's a "<u>beastie</u>" on the island is suggested by a <u>littlun</u>. At first the older boys just laugh, but <u>gradually</u> they start to <u>believe</u> that there's something to be <u>afraid</u> of.

> Golding uses the <u>symbol</u> of the <u>beast</u> to introduce the idea of <u>fear</u>. As more boys start to <u>believe</u> in it, the <u>atmosphere</u> becomes more <u>terrifying</u>.

2) <u>Simon's</u> comment that the boys <u>scream</u> in their <u>sleep</u> "As if it wasn't a <u>good</u> island" <u>foreshadows</u> the horrible things that happen <u>later</u> on.

3) As the boys become more <u>frightened</u>, they act more <u>savagely</u>. This makes them more <u>scared</u>, because they think the <u>beast</u> is getting <u>stronger</u>. When they kill <u>Simon</u> with "<u>teeth</u> and <u>claws</u>", Golding is showing how <u>fear</u> has made them behave like <u>wild animals</u>.

Fear of the beast isn't rational

1) <u>Descriptions</u> of the beast keep <u>changing</u> — the reader knows early on that it <u>only</u> exists in the boys' <u>imagination</u>.

2) The three most <u>rational</u> characters — Ralph, Piggy and Simon — try to <u>convince</u> the others that the beast <u>doesn't</u> exist:

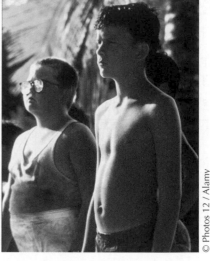

© Photos 12 / Alamy

> • Ralph says that they need to <u>talk</u> about their <u>fear</u>, and <u>agree</u> that there's <u>no reason</u> to be scared.
>
> • Piggy says life "is <u>scientific</u>" and the beast doesn't exist.
>
> • Simon suggests that the only thing they should fear is the <u>evil</u> in human nature — maybe the beast is "<u>only us</u>".

3) They don't realise how <u>strong</u> the boys' <u>fear</u> is — it's stronger than their <u>ability</u> to <u>think logically</u>.

Jack uses the others' fear to control their behaviour

> Golding doesn't make it <u>clear</u> how much Jack <u>believes</u> in the beast, and how much he just uses it to <u>control</u> the others. He says it's "a <u>hunter</u>" — perhaps deep down he sees that it <u>represents</u> his <u>dark</u> side.

1) Jack <u>encourages</u> others to <u>join</u> his tribe by saying that his hunters will <u>protect</u> them from the beast.

2) He tells them that the beast can <u>disguise</u> itself and that they can <u>never really kill it</u>. This <u>keeps</u> them feeling <u>insecure</u> and <u>threatened</u>, which increases Jack's <u>power</u> over them.

KEY QUOTE

"But I tell you there isn't a beast!"

The boys are scared stiff of the dead airman — they think he's the beast. Nope, just a rotting dead guy, nowt to be scared of. Golding uses the scary backdrop of nuclear war to show that life is full of fear and conflict.

Section Three — Themes

Power and Leadership

This is a big theme in the book — who's in charge. Ralph versus Jack. Civilisation versus savagery. Rules versus fun. Good versus evil. Spider-Man versus the Green Goblin. No wait, scrap that one.

Power changes hands through the novel

1) When the boys first land, they want a society that's similar to what they're used to — they focus on rescue and rules, so Ralph's leadership style appeals to them.

2) As they become more savage, their desires become more basic — they want food, safety and certainty. Jack's dictatorial leadership style appeals now — he gives them meat and tells them what to do so they don't have to think for themselves.

Ralph and Jack represent two very different leadership styles — democracy and dictatorship.

Ralph is the closest they have to an adult leader

1) Ralph is a responsible leader. He uses his power to protect people — he stands up for Piggy and tries to look after the littluns. He would like to have fun, but he has a sense of duty to the others.

2) Ralph wants them to live by the rules because they're the "only thing we've got" — the only thing that links them to their old lives.

3) He doubts his own ability to lead the group — he wishes he could think like Piggy. This is another reminder that he's just a child.

> **Symbolism**
>
> The conch symbolises authority and Ralph's democratic leadership.

4) He becomes disillusioned at how difficult it is to keep people focused on unpopular tasks. The others boys don't see how important it is to have shelters and a signal fire to link them to civilisation.

Jack's leadership is violent and irresponsible

1) Jack craves power, but he doesn't want the responsibility that comes with it.

2) Jack's not democratically elected — he challenges Ralph's power and eventually steals it from him.

3) As Jack becomes more powerful he also becomes more vicious. Without adult control, he's free to enforce obedience in fairly violent ways. He becomes a dictator who abuses his power.

4) Jack's power, maintained through violence and fear, is symbolised by a stick sharpened at both ends.

> The stick sharpened at both ends could hurt the hunter as well as the prey. It symbolises the fact that the society that Jack has created is self-destructive.

© United Archives GmbH / Alamy

Show you understand the different types of power...

Make it clear to the examiner that you know the differences between Ralph's and Jack's styles of leadership. You could even link this to context — e.g. parallels can be made between Jack and Adolf Hitler (see p.48).

Section Three — Themes

Nature

The setting of the novel is a beautiful tropical island, and that lovely green scenery actually becomes a theme of the novel. The main thing the boys do with it though is totally mess it up. Nasty boys.

The island is a tropical paradise

1) In *Lord of the Flies*, Golding uses detailed <u>descriptions</u> of the setting to create <u>atmosphere</u>:

   - There's a <u>sandy beach</u>, <u>palm trees</u> and a <u>pool</u> to swim in — it's like a giant <u>playground</u>.
   - The lagoon is <u>calm</u>, <u>beautiful</u> and <u>safe</u> — the descriptions of it sound almost <u>magical</u>.
   - There's <u>fresh water</u> and plenty of <u>fruit</u> — it should be <u>easy</u> to <u>survive</u> there.

2) The <u>island</u> is like the <u>Garden of Eden</u> — the perfect place in the <u>Bible</u> where Adam and Eve live until they <u>learn about good and evil</u> and lose their innocence. In the novel, the boys learn about the good and evil <u>inside themselves</u>, and by the end, their <u>innocence is lost</u> too.

Nature isn't always friendly

1) At the beginning of the story, Ralph and Piggy have <u>already</u> been <u>scratched</u> by thorns and Piggy gets <u>tangled</u> in creepers. Golding is hinting that the island <u>isn't</u> a perfect setting.

2) The boys eat <u>fruit</u> that's either <u>not ripe</u> enough, or <u>too ripe</u> — this gives them "<u>chronic diarrhoea</u>".

3) The <u>weather</u> often reflects the <u>mood</u> of the story — on the night Simon dies in the <u>wild</u> and <u>frantic</u> dance, the weather is also <u>wild</u> and <u>thundery</u>.

4) In the ocean, "<u>sharks waited</u>" — the boys are <u>trapped</u> on the island. This introduces a feeling of <u>danger</u>.

© iStockphoto.com / Katherine Moffitt

The boys damage the island — but nature repairs itself

1) The <u>crashing plane</u> left a "long scar" in the forest. It's as if the island has been <u>injured</u>.

2) Nature is <u>indifferent</u> to human behaviour — a storm drags the plane wreckage out to sea, and undergrowth begins to cover up the scar left by the crash. It's the <u>boys</u>, not the island, who will <u>never</u> be the <u>same</u> again.

3) The boys' first <u>fire</u> destroys a large area of forest, burning their <u>firewood</u> and the <u>fruit</u> trees. They use <u>fire</u> as a <u>weapon</u> at the end of the novel, and the island becomes "burning wreckage".

> The boys' <u>destruction</u> of the island <u>symbolises</u> man's destruction of <u>nature</u>.

EXAM TIP

Write about the way Golding uses the natural world...

It's much more than just a pretty island, you know. The examiner will be impressed if you can write about how Golding uses the setting to create mood and atmosphere, such as on the night of Simon's murder.

Games

Games are a pretty important theme, considering it's a game that eventually leads to Simon's murder. Even when the boys are talking about scary violent stuff, they use words like "fun" and "play" — it's quite creepy...

The boys play innocent games at first

At the beginning of the novel, the boys act as they would at home, playing happily and exploring. Golding is emphasising that the boys are just young children:

- Ralph and the others dive and swim in the lagoon. The littluns build sand castles.

- They hold an election for chief, but it still feels like a game. The voting's just a "toy".

- Exploring the island is exciting for them. They don't think about long-term survival. Ralph says they can get food and "have fun" "until the grown-ups come to fetch us".

Violence soon creeps in

© Columbia/Everett/Rex Features

1) The littluns try to replace the civilisation they've lost by building sand castles surrounded by "tracks, walls, railway lines". Roger and Maurice destroy them, which shows their rejection of civilisation.

2) As the group gets more savage, the hunting dances change from games into something more violent. After Robert is hurt, Jack jokingly suggests they use a littlun next time because they want to kill their prey. This foreshadows Simon's death in the next dance.

3) In Chapter Four, Roger makes a game of throwing stones at a littlun, but makes sure he doesn't hurt him. By Chapter Eleven he's throwing them to hurt Ralph and Piggy — this game reaches a climax when he rolls the boulder that kills Piggy.

The games become serious by the end of the book

1) In Chapter Eleven, Ralph and Piggy assume that Jack's games are still bound by morals and that he'll give Piggy's glasses back because it's "right". They don't see that he no longer cares about "playing the game".

2) When the tribe hunts Ralph, he wishes he could say to them "I've got pax", like schoolboys would to pause a game. He knows it wouldn't work though. It's a sign that their childhood innocence is lost.

3) The naval officer describes the hunt as "Fun and games". He thinks they're playing a childish game of war — but their war is as real and deadly as the one the adults are involved in.

Link games to a loss of innocence...

Kids like to play games. Nice games like hide and seek. But don't just write that in the exam. Explain how the increasing violence of the boys' games in the novel shows that they're losing their childhood innocence.

Evil

This page is on eeeeevil. The book leaves you wondering whether Jack and Roger are just naturally evil or whether all humans are capable of evil behaviour if they're put in that sort of situation. It's a tricky one...

Golding uses darkness to represent evil

1) At the beginning of the novel, the <u>choir</u> is described as "something dark... fumbling along". The choir becomes Jack's <u>tribe</u>. The evil in human nature takes a <u>physical form</u> when they hunt and kill.

2) In the <u>dark</u> the younger boys have terrible <u>nightmares</u> which lead to their fear of the <u>beast</u>.

3) Simon is murdered on a dark night. The darkness <u>panics</u> the boys into thinking he's <u>the beast</u>.

4) Ralph <u>weeps</u> at the end of the novel for the "<u>darkness</u> of man's heart". The <u>naval officer's</u> smart <u>white</u> uniform <u>hides</u> the truth that Ralph now <u>understands</u> — that <u>evil</u> exists within all human beings.

Some characters have stronger evil instincts than others

1) <u>Jack's</u> obsessed with hunting and <u>killing</u>. He leads most of the <u>violent</u> events in the story.

2) <u>Roger</u> likes <u>destroying</u> things. At first it's just <u>sand castles</u>, but by the end he's become an <u>executioner</u>. He kills Piggy in <u>cold blood</u> because Piggy points out how <u>savage</u> the boys' behaviour has become.

3) <u>Piggy</u> and <u>Ralph</u> usually show the <u>good</u> side of human nature. They <u>recognise</u> their <u>evil instincts</u> and try to <u>contain</u> them. This suggests that evil can be <u>suppressed</u> by following society's <u>moral rules</u>.

4) <u>Simon's</u> the boy with <u>least</u> evil in him, but his goodness is <u>overpowered</u> by the evil in the others.

The pig's head on a stick means several things

1) The <u>pig's head</u> is left as an offering for the beast — it represents the boys' <u>fear</u>.

2) It tells Simon "<u>I'm part of you</u>" — Golding is showing that there's no "<u>beast</u>" — it's their own <u>fear</u> that causes the <u>evil</u> inside them to emerge.

3) The pig's head is called the "<u>Lord of the Flies</u>", which is what the name of the <u>demon</u> Beelzebub means. When it speaks to Simon, it's like the voice of <u>evil</u> talking:

Courtesy of Janus Films

- It sounds very <u>cynical</u> — it knows it will always <u>win</u>.
- It speaks with "the voice of a <u>schoolmaster</u>" — Simon is realising that the <u>adult</u> world is <u>corrupt</u> too.

4) When Ralph's being <u>hunted</u>, he <u>breaks</u> the Lord of the Flies and <u>uses the stick</u>. He destroys the <u>symbol of evil</u>, but he's <u>prepared to attack</u> the others — this shows that he's been <u>corrupted by evil</u>.

KEY QUOTE

"I'd like to put on war-paint and be a savage."

Ralph recognises that he's tempted by the evil within him, but this is overpowered by his desire to "keep the fire burning" — we may all be capable of evil, but perhaps it's possible to choose to be civilised.

Practice Questions

This section was quite hard if you ask me — the stuff you've got to learn here isn't exactly obvious if you're not used to analysing books. My advice to you is to just get really familiar with the whole book — read it again and again so you know who says what and when. Anyway, to begin with, let's see what you've remembered from this section. The quick questions should be just that — quick. The in-depth questions should take you a little bit longer — try to write a paragraph or so for each one.

Quick Questions

1) Give two examples of the boys living by civilised rules from their old life early on in the novel.

2) Give an example of one of the first acts of violence in the book.

3) What does the conch symbolise? What is being symbolised when it gets smashed?

4) Give one example of a minor act of violence which the boys consider to be a game.

5) Give an example from the book of darkness as a sign of evil.

In-depth Questions

1) Why do you think Piggy is so keen to protect the rules?

2) Do you think the stick sharpened at both ends is a fitting symbol of Jack's leadership? Why?

3) In what ways is clothing important in *Lord of the Flies*?

4) How do innocent games become corrupted in *Lord of the Flies*?

5) How is Ralph's response to the littluns' early fear of the beast different from Jack's? Explain your answer.

Practice Questions

Now on to the tougher stuff — but hopefully not too tough. Don't rush through these questions — take your time and use them wisely. Practising exam-style questions now will improve your chances of getting those sparkly top grades in the real thing.

Exam-style Questions

1) How does Golding express ideas about democracy and dictatorship in *Lord of the Flies*?

2) How are the settings in the novel important to its ideas and themes?

3) Write about how Golding uses the symbols of the conch and the Lord of the Flies to get across important ideas in the novel.

4) How does Golding present the figure of the beast in *Lord of the Flies*?

5) 'While it appears that evil does triumph at the end of *Lord of the Flies*, the view of human nature depicted in the novel isn't entirely negative.'
   To what extent do you agree with this statement?

Structure and Viewpoint of 'Lord of the Flies'

This section is all about the techniques Golding used to make *Lord of the Flies* as good as it is.
First, how the book's written — the way it's organised and the points of view it uses.

You could split the story into three main stages

1) At first the boys <u>explore</u> and try to be <u>organised</u>. Ralph is in charge and <u>civilised values</u> are still important.

> Golding twists the normal <u>structure</u> of <u>adventure</u> stories — the boys are <u>rescued</u>, but they're not <u>saved</u> from their new <u>knowledge</u> of their own <u>evil</u>.

2) Next, their <u>fear of the beast</u> gets stronger. Jack breaks away to set up a <u>new tribe</u>.

3) After this, the <u>murders</u> begin. The boys reach their most <u>primitive</u> level just before the grown-ups arrive.

We're not sure how long the story takes

1) The boys don't <u>keep track</u> of time. There are only <u>clues</u> about how <u>long</u> the story takes, such as the boys' "<u>long hair</u>", the <u>decomposition</u> of the airman's body, and the fact that they <u>forget</u> about their <u>old life</u>.

2) Losing track of time <u>symbolises</u> their abandonment of the <u>civilised</u> world. <u>Piggy's</u> suggestion that they build a <u>sundial</u> shows that he's still <u>clinging</u> to science and the <u>old life</u>.

The viewpoint of the novel changes

1) The story sometimes follows <u>individual</u> characters and sometimes the <u>whole group</u>.

WHOLE GROUP
1) Some dramatic incidents involve the <u>whole group</u> — like the <u>fire</u> getting out of control, and Simon and Piggy's <u>deaths</u>.
2) Some events are <u>repeated</u> to show how things are <u>changing</u>. Each <u>assembly</u> has a slightly different <u>mood</u>. The <u>hunts</u> also become more and more <u>violent</u>.

INDIVIDUALS
1) <u>Jack</u> sometimes <u>hunts</u> alone.
2) <u>Ralph</u> sometimes sits alone — trying to <u>work out</u> how to deal with the others.
3) <u>Simon</u> looks for <u>quiet places</u> to <u>think</u>.

Following an individual character allows the reader to get inside their head and understand their feelings and actions.

2) At other times the story doesn't <u>focus</u> on the <u>boys</u>, e.g. at the start of Chapter Six there's a battle above the island. This is a reminder that the <u>outside world</u> is as <u>dangerous</u> and troubled as the island.

3) The novel <u>switches</u> to an <u>adult</u> perspective when the <u>naval officer</u> arrives. He sees "<u>little boys</u>" <u>playing</u> at war, while Golding has <u>persuaded</u> the reader that they're "<u>savages</u>" on a <u>deadly hunt</u>.

Comment on how Golding uses viewpoints in the novel...

Have a think about why Golding narrates different events from the point of view of different characters. For example, focusing on Ralph while he's being hunted really emphasises how scared and alone he is.

How the Characters Speak

The boys' language gets worse through the book, which shows their increasing savagery. (If you're lucky you can write swear words in your exam. As part of making a good, relevant point about the novel of course...)

At first the boys sound well spoken

© Geoffrey Robinson/Rex Features

1) The boys say things like "Wacco", "Wizard" and "Whizzoh" to show how excited they are. It's the sort of slang that public schoolboys would use in the 1950s. It makes them seem very innocent.

2) They sometimes sound like comic-book characters. They use words like "Bong!" and "Doink!" as they imagine punishing rule breakers. Cartoon violence like this is unreal — they have no idea that they're capable of real violence.

Their language changes as their society does

1) As their society becomes more savage, so does their language. They begin to swear more, and use coarser language, especially when they are angry or excited, e.g. Jack shouts "Bollocks to the rules!" The boys enjoy their freedom from the normal conventions of politeness.

2) After the first pig hunt, they start up a violent chant — "*Kill the pig. Cut her throat. Spill her blood.*" This chant brings the boys together as a mob without individual responsibility. This lets them perform savage acts that they'd never do individually.

3) The boys do a lot of shouting and whooping when they're excited. These sounds get less human and more chilling as their behaviour gets more violent. When they're hunting Ralph, they make a "ululation" (a howling noise) which immediately dies away when they see the naval officer. He's a sudden reminder of the civilisation that they've abandoned.

The way the boys speak shows their characters

1) Jack gives a lot of commands. He gives his opinions in an arrogant and forceful way, e.g. when he says "I ought to be chief". He's used to being a leader, and has an aggressive personality.

2) Ralph sometimes struggles to explain himself. He knows he needs to speak clearly to the assembly to help them understand. He tries to be a leader, but his language is sometimes childish, e.g. when he claims that his dad will rescue them. Golding is reminding the reader that even the leaders are just children.

3) Piggy's way of talking shows that he's different. He isn't as well-spoken as the others, and says things like "Them fruit". He starts a lot of sentences with "My auntie", which shows how he clings to the adult world.

"Choir! Stand still!"

From the very beginning of the novel, it's clear from Jack's language that he's very commanding and likes to be the boss. And island life doesn't exactly mellow him — his language is aggressive throughout the novel.

Imagery and Symbolism

There's a lot more to writing than just telling the story — that would be pretty boring. Writers also use imagery and symbolism to create different meanings and effects. Here's how Golding does it...

There are lots of symbols in the novel

1) The <u>conch</u> is a symbol of <u>authority</u> and <u>democracy</u> — only the boy holding it is allowed to speak. Initially, all the boys <u>respect</u> the conch, but it's <u>destroyed</u> in Chapter Eleven — this represents the <u>end of democracy</u> on the island.

2) The <u>signal fire</u> symbolises the boys' <u>hope of rescue</u>. Ralph and Piggy recognise the <u>importance</u> of the fire throughout, whereas Jack quickly <u>loses interest</u> — this reflects their <u>different views</u> on rescue. Ironically, it is the fire that Jack's tribe light to <u>kill</u> Ralph that brings help — this could symbolise the victory of <u>savagery</u> over <u>civilisation</u>.

3) Ralph and Jack's <u>opposing viewpoints</u> are symbolised by the things they believe are important. Ralph focuses on building <u>shelters</u>, which represent <u>civilisation</u>, while Jack is only interested in <u>hunting</u>, which represents <u>savagery</u>.

There are other symbols too — e.g. the pig's head represents fear (see p. 40), and Piggy's glasses symbolise reason (see p. 34).

The names used in the book are symbolic

1) At the start the boys are "<u>children</u>" and their meeting is an "<u>assembly</u>". By the end of the book the group is called "the tribe" and each child is a "<u>savage</u>". This symbolises the fact that they've lost their <u>identities</u> and are no longer <u>innocent</u>. When the naval officer sees them they become "<u>little boys</u>" again.

2) At first, <u>Jack</u> wants to be called by his <u>surname</u> to show he's not a "kid". By the end of the novel he's "<u>the Chief</u>" — he's <u>lost his identity</u> and defines himself by how much <u>power</u> he has over the other boys.

3) <u>Piggy's</u> name represents his status as a <u>victim</u> — like the pigs on the island.

Descriptive language and imagery create atmosphere

1) <u>Descriptions</u> of the <u>beauty</u> of the island create a <u>peaceful atmosphere</u> and <u>slow down</u> the <u>action</u>.

2) Sometimes the language is full of <u>horror</u>. For example, the pig's head on a stick "grinned and dripped" and its <u>guts</u> are "a black blob of flies that buzzed like a saw". These descriptions suggest <u>evil</u>.

3) <u>Piggy's</u> death is <u>shocking</u> because it is described so <u>simply</u>. As Piggy falls onto the rocks, "His <u>head opened</u> and stuff came out and turned red." This gets across to the reader Ralph's <u>horror</u> and <u>disbelief</u>.

> Golding uses foreshadowing to build suspense, e.g. the boys <u>playing the part</u> of the pig in the hunting dance foreshadows Simon's <u>murder</u>.

4) As the boys become <u>more savage</u>, Golding uses <u>animal imagery</u> to show how <u>inhuman</u> they've become, e.g. when Jack first <u>paints</u> his face his laughter turns to a "<u>bloodthirsty snarling</u>".

5) Simon is murdered with "the tearing of <u>teeth</u> and <u>claws</u>". Their <u>animal instincts</u> have taken over from their <u>civilised</u> lives.

KEY QUOTE

"ape-like among the tangle of trees."

Golding uses animalistic language to show how Jack's becoming less human. He reacts to a sudden noise like a startled "ape", with "a hiss of indrawn breath". Now what was Simon saying about the beast within...

Practice Questions

It's the moment you've been waiting for — yep, it's time to test your knowledge of all the clever techniques Golding used to make 'Lord of the Flies' such a gripping read. On your marks... get set... go.

Quick Questions

1) Give an example of a time in the book when the story is focused on something other than the boys.

2) Give two examples of words that the boys use that make them sound like public schoolboys.

3) What happens to the language of the boys as they lose their grip on civilised behaviour?

4) Piggy's way of speaking marks him out as being different. Describe how Piggy speaks.

5) Give an example of some language used in the book that is vivid and full of horror.

In-depth Questions

1) We're not told how long the events of the novel last. Why do you think that is?

2) The effects of the island's weather are described in detail, for example at the beginning of Chapter Four. Why do you think Golding does this?

3) How does Golding use symbolism to explore the conflict between civilisation and savagery?

4) When Piggy dies "His head opened and stuff came out and turned red". Why do you think Golding uses such simple language in this sentence?

5) Look at the language Golding uses to describe Simon's body being washed out to sea in Chapter Nine. Why do you think he uses this language?

Practice Questions

Now it's time for some exam-style questions. Pick your favourite one first and when you've finished answering it, have a look back at the section to see if you've missed out anything important.

Exam-style Questions

1) Read the description of Simon's murder near the end of Chapter Nine from, "He ran stumbling through..." to "...staining the sand".
   How does Golding create an atmosphere of fear in this passage?

2) Choose one passage from *Lord of the Flies* that vividly describes the island.
   What methods does Golding use to bring his descriptions to life?

3) How effective is the first chapter of *Lord of the Flies* at introducing themes that Golding develops in the rest of the novel?

4) How does Golding make hunting so important in the novel?

5) Choose a passage from the novel that you find particularly tense or exciting.
   What techniques does Golding use to build suspense in this passage?

Historical Background to 'Lord of the Flies'

Lord of the Flies was written in the 1950s. If you understand what was going on in the world then, you'll have a better understanding of what influenced Golding and what he's hinting at in the book.

Golding was deeply affected by World War Two

1) <u>Germany</u> was led into World War Two by the <u>Nazi</u> party — an extreme <u>anti-Jewish</u> party who rose to power in the early 1930s. The <u>Nazis</u> committed terrible <u>crimes</u> during the war — they were responsible for the <u>holocaust</u> (the slaughter of <u>millions</u> of Jews and people of other minorities).

2) This made Golding <u>pessimistic</u> about human nature — he believed that <u>evil</u> couldn't be <u>defeated</u>, because it's <u>inside everyone</u>. There are <u>parallels</u> between the <u>Nazi party</u> and the <u>characters</u> in *Lord of the Flies*:

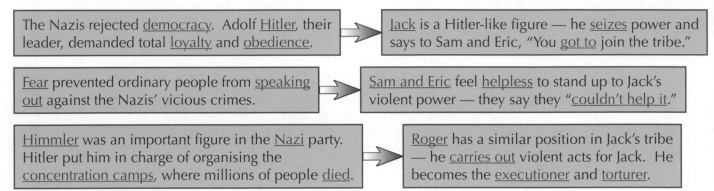

The Nazis rejected <u>democracy</u>. Adolf <u>Hitler</u>, their leader, demanded total <u>loyalty</u> and <u>obedience</u>.	<u>Jack</u> is a Hitler-like figure — he <u>seizes</u> power and says to Sam and Eric, "You <u>got to</u> join the tribe."
<u>Fear</u> prevented ordinary people from <u>speaking out</u> against the Nazis' vicious crimes.	<u>Sam and Eric</u> feel <u>helpless</u> to stand up to Jack's violent power — they say they "<u>couldn't help it</u>."
<u>Himmler</u> was an important figure in the <u>Nazi</u> party. Hitler put him in charge of organising the <u>concentration camps</u>, where millions of people <u>died</u>.	<u>Roger</u> has a similar position in Jack's tribe — he <u>carries out</u> violent acts for Jack. He becomes the <u>executioner</u> and <u>torturer</u>.

After the war there was tension between the USSR and the West

1) The <u>USSR</u> (the Soviet Union) and the <u>USA</u> had fought together in World War Two, but they <u>disagreed</u> about how to <u>divide up</u> Europe afterwards. They also had very different <u>political beliefs</u> — America was a <u>democracy</u>, and the USSR was a <u>communist</u> dictatorship. This led to almost <u>fifty years</u> of <u>hostility</u> between the two states — the <u>Cold War</u>.

2) Both sides had huge stocks of <u>nuclear weapons</u> — they thought that having the most weapons would <u>protect</u> them from being attacked. If conflict had <u>broken out</u>, it could have <u>destroyed</u> the <u>world</u>.

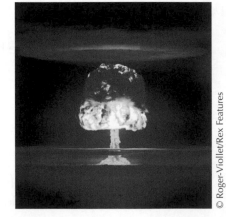
© Roger-Viollet/Rex Features

- The <u>conflict</u> between Ralph and Jack is like the <u>tension</u> between America and the USSR. Ralph represents <u>democracy</u>, and Jack represents <u>dictatorship</u>.
- When conflict <u>breaks out</u>, the resulting fire <u>destroys</u> the island — it becomes a "burning wreckage".

'Lord of the Flies' is set during a nuclear war

1) Piggy reminds Ralph that the plane <u>crashed</u> because they were <u>attacked</u>. Piggy asks Ralph if he remembers what the pilot said "About the <u>atom bomb</u>? <u>They're all dead</u>."

2) The dead airman comes from a "<u>battle</u> fought at ten miles' height".

3) This creates a backdrop of <u>fear</u> and <u>violence</u> that echoes the fear and violence on the <u>island</u>. At the end the boys are <u>rescued</u>, but Golding makes it clear that they're going back to a <u>savage</u>, <u>war-torn</u> society.

Historical Background to 'Lord of the Flies'

You thought the history lesson was over didn't you? Hard cheese — there's a bit more to learn. Actually, I think this history stuff's pretty interesting. It's like stepping back in time for a nose about.

Being British used to mean being in charge

1) In the 1950s, Britain still had a large empire across the world. For hundreds of years, British forces had been moving into countries and taking over, building up the British Empire. The boys treat the island in a similar way. Ralph says confidently, "This belongs to us", and the boys "savoured the right of domination".

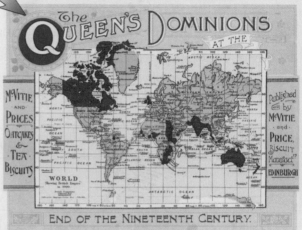

2) Being British implied certain standards and values. Jack says "We're English; and the English are best at everything." Their behaviour later on in the story challenges this idea.

3) When the book was written, the British Armed Forces were no longer such a supreme power. Ralph has total confidence that his father, who is in the Navy, will come to rescue them, but Piggy points out that nobody knows where they are.

4) The British Empire had begun to break up by the 1950s — in the novel, the boys' society breaks into pieces.

© Mary Evans Picture Library

Social class was important in Britain in the 1950s

A lot of people believed that a privileged background and good schooling automatically produced decent human beings. Golding shows that this might not be true.

BACKGROUND

1) The boys are from middle- and upper-class backgrounds, and have had orderly, respectable upbringings. They would be expected to be self-disciplined and reasonable at home.

2) Their savage behaviour by the end of the story shows that these values aren't instinctive. The boys could only keep violence under control while they had to obey outside rules.

3) Piggy is less posh than the other boys — he says things like "Aren't I having none?". But he turns out to be one of the nicest, most intelligent characters. Golding is showing that social class doesn't determine how good or worthwhile a person is.

SCHOOLING

4) Jack and the choir seem to have come from an elite public school. They wear a formal uniform and use words like "matins" (morning prayer) and "precentor" (choir teacher). The boys would have had a very strict hierarchy, and a controlled existence.

5) The strict discipline hasn't given them self-control though. It has just made them more likely to obey a vicious leader like Jack and enjoy being wild for a change.

EXAM TIP

Think about the importance of the characters' backgrounds...

If you know your stuff about the boys' social class, it'll help you better understand their characters and Golding's message that all humans are capable of evil under the right circumstances. Except me, I'm nice.

50

Adventure Stories

Golding used the adventure story genre as his inspiration, but he decided to change it a bit. He didn't just want to entertain his readers — he wanted to give them a message about humanity.

Many boys' adventure books were set on tropical islands

1) At first, the boys <u>imagine</u> themselves as <u>heroes</u> in an <u>adventure</u> story — they mention *Treasure Island* and *Swallows and Amazons*, both about exciting <u>adventures</u> on islands.

2) Golding also refers to *<u>The Coral Island</u>* by R. M. Ballantyne — Ralph <u>thinks</u> the island will be "a coral island" "leaping into real life", and he's <u>excited</u> at the idea of "<u>No grown-ups</u>!"

3) *The Coral Island* is about three <u>British</u> boys who are <u>shipwrecked</u> on a tropical island and have incredible <u>adventures</u>.

> Golding <u>deliberately</u> used the same <u>names</u> as in *<u>The Coral Island</u>* (Ralph and Jack). He wanted to write a more <u>realistic</u> version.

Golding's story is more realistic than other stories

Here's how *Lord of the Flies* <u>compares</u> to *The Coral Island*, which it's loosely based on:

The Coral Island	Lord of the Flies
The boys light their <u>fire</u> by rubbing two sticks together. They have all the <u>skills</u> they need.	At first, Jack and Ralph <u>don't</u> know how to light a fire without <u>matches</u>. Jack eventually uses Piggy's <u>glasses</u>.
Jack is a <u>natural leader</u>. He always knows what to do and is brave, decent and fair. There is <u>no conflict</u> between him and Ralph — just friendship and support.	Jack and Ralph start to become <u>friends</u> but they have very different personalities and values. This soon causes <u>conflict</u> between them which turns to <u>hatred</u>.
The boys kill a pig with <u>hardly</u> any noise or mess.	The killing of the mother pig is <u>bloody</u> and <u>grotesque</u>.

'Lord of the Flies' made people think

1) Books like *The Coral Island* often portrayed <u>native people</u> who behaved in <u>brutal</u> ways, and British people who were very <u>civilised</u>. Golding challenges these <u>stereotypes</u>, showing British schoolboys behaving in a barbaric way — they're very capable of <u>savage behaviour</u>.

2) In *Lord of the Flies*, there are <u>no enemies</u> such as pirates or cannibals to fight. The boys encounter <u>evil</u> from within <u>themselves</u>. This makes it much more <u>difficult</u> to come to terms with.

"Jolly good show. Like the Coral Island."

The naval officer who arrives on the island at the end of the novel assumes that the boys' experience must've been something like *The Coral Island* — all jolly "fun and games". Oh, how wrong he was...

Practice Questions

So you think you've finished this section, eh? Well, before you go wandering off to more interesting things, stretch your brain with these questions. As always, check back through the section if you get stuck on anything — you need to be able to answer them all.

Quick Questions

1) Which German dictator can Jack's leadership be compared to?

2) Who can Roger be compared to?
   a) Stalin
   b) Darth Vader
   c) Himmler

3) Which post-World War Two conflict does the tension between Jack and Ralph represent?

4) How can you tell that a nuclear war is going on in *Lord of the Flies*?

5) What was happening to the British Empire in the 1950s?

6) Which boy seems to come from a lower social class than the others?

7) Which boys seem to have come from an elite public school?

8) What is the name of the book that *Lord of the Flies* is loosely based on?

9) True or false — *Lord of the Flies* was written as a more optimistic version of the book in Q8?

10) Is there any evidence that the boys themselves have read adventure stories set on tropical islands?

Practice Questions

Here are some in-depth questions and some exam-style questions for you to have a go at. I can't guarantee they'll be loads of fun (or even a small amount of fun) but you'll feel a lot more confident in the exam if you've done lots of practice questions. Ready... steady... unleash those question-answering skills.

In-depth Questions

1) Do you think Golding's experiences in World War Two had an influence on Chapter One? Why?

2) Do you think Golding believed that moral, civilised behaviour is linked to social class? Explain your answer.

3) Do you think that the story of *Lord of the Flies* is more realistic than a traditional desert island adventure story such as *The Coral Island*? Why?

4) Do you find the violence in the novel more shocking because it comes from children rather than adults? Why?

Exam-style Questions

1) How does Golding express ideas about war and conflict in *Lord of the Flies*?

2) 'The events of the novel suggest that Golding had a negative view of humanity.' How far do you agree with this statement?

3) How does Golding challenge traditional ideas about class and Britishness in *Lord of the Flies*?

Exam Preparation

Getting to know the text will put you at a massive advantage in the exam. It's not enough just to read it though — you've got to get to grips with the nitty-gritty bits. It's all about gathering evidence...

The exam questions will test four main skills

You will need to show the examiner that you can:

1) Write about the text in a thoughtful way — picking out appropriate examples and quotations to back up your opinions.

2) Identify and explain features of the text's form, structure and language. Show how the author uses these to create meanings and effects.

3) Relate the text to its cultural, social and historical background.

   Not all exam boards will test you on this. Check with your teacher.

4) Write in a clear, well-structured way. 5% of the marks in your English Literature exams are for spelling, punctuation and grammar. Make sure that your writing is as accurate as possible.

Preparation is important

1) It's important to cover all the different sections of this book in your revision. You need to make sure you understand the text's context, plot, characters, themes and writer's techniques.

2) In the exam, you'll need to bring together your ideas about these topics to answer the question quickly.

3) Think about the different characters and themes in the text, and write down some key points and ideas about each one. Then, find some evidence to support each point — this could be something from any of the sections in this book. You could set out your evidence in a table like this:

Theme: Fear	
Symbolism	Beast represents boys' fear. As more boys believe in it, they become more scared and more savage.
Human nature	Simon suggests that the beast is "only us" — evil is inside them and they should fear themselves.
Animalistic language	Fear makes the boys behave like animals — they kill Simon with "teeth and claws".
Power	Jack uses boys' fear of the beast to control them — says the beast can't be killed so they'll want his protection.
Context of war	Mentions of nuclear war in the novel (e.g. "atom bomb") reflect the Cold War — there's fear in everyday life.

Preparing to succeed — a cunning plot indeed...

Knowing the plot inside out will be unbelievably helpful in the exam. It'll help you to stay calm and make sure you write a brilliant answer that positively glitters with little gems of evidence. The exam's just a chance for you to show off...

The Exam Question

This page deals with how to approach an exam question. The stuff below will help you get started on a scorching exam answer, more scorching than, say, a phoenix cooking fiery fajitas in a flaming furnace.

Read the question carefully and underline key words

1) The style of question you'll get depends on which <u>exam board</u> you're taking.

2) Read all the <u>instructions</u> carefully. Make sure you know <u>how many</u> questions you need to answer and <u>how much time</u> you should spend answering each one.

3) If the question has <u>more than one part</u>, look at the total number of marks for each bit. This should help you to plan your <u>time</u> in the exam.

4) <u>Read</u> the question at least <u>twice</u> so you completely understand it. <u>Underline</u> the key words. If you're given an <u>extract</u>, underline <u>important</u> words or phrases in that too.

Henry didn't read the weather report carefully enough when planning his weekend activities.

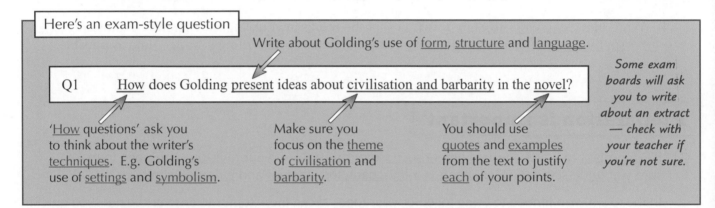

Here's an exam-style question

Write about Golding's use of <u>form</u>, <u>structure</u> and <u>language</u>.

Q1   <u>How</u> does Golding <u>present</u> ideas about <u>civilisation and barbarity</u> in the <u>novel</u>?

Some exam boards will ask you to write about an extract — check with your teacher if you're not sure.

'<u>How</u> questions' ask you to think about the writer's <u>techniques</u>. E.g. Golding's use of <u>settings</u> and <u>symbolism</u>.

Make sure you focus on the <u>theme</u> of <u>civilisation</u> and <u>barbarity</u>.

You should use <u>quotes</u> and <u>examples</u> from the text to justify <u>each</u> of your points.

Get to know exam language

Some <u>words</u> come up time and again in <u>exam questions</u>. Have a look at some <u>specimen</u> questions, pick out words that are <u>often used</u> in questions and make sure that you <u>understand</u> what they mean. You could <u>write a few down</u> whilst you're revising. For example:

Question Word	You need to...
Explore / Explain	Show <u>how</u> the writer deals with a <u>theme</u>, <u>character</u> or <u>idea</u>. Make several <u>different</u> points to answer the question.
How does	Think about the <u>techniques</u> or <u>literary features</u> that the author uses to get their point across.
Give examples	Use <u>direct quotes</u> and describe <u>events</u> from the text in your own words.
Refer to	Read the question so that you know if you need to write about just an <u>extract</u>, or an extract and the <u>rest of the text</u>.

The advice squad — the best cops in the NYPD...

Whatever question you're asked in the exam, your answer should touch on the main characters, themes, structure and language of the text. All the stuff we've covered in the rest of the book in fact. It's so neat, it's almost like we planned it.

Planning Your Answer

I'll say this once — and then I'll probably repeat it several times — it is absolutely, completely, totally and utterly essential that you make a plan before you start writing. Only a fool jumps right in without a plan...

Plan your answer before you start

1) If you plan, you're less likely to forget something <u>important</u>.

2) A good plan will help you <u>organise</u> your ideas — and write a good, <u>well-structured</u> essay.

3) Write your plan at the <u>top of your answer booklet</u> and draw a <u>neat line</u> through it when you've finished.

4) <u>Don't</u> spend <u>too long</u> on your plan. It's only <u>rough work</u>, so you don't need to write in full sentences. Here are a few <u>examples</u> of different ways you can plan your answer:

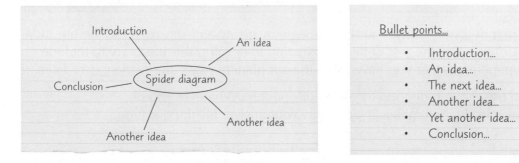

Include bits of evidence in your plan

1) <u>Writing</u> your essay will be much <u>easier</u> if you include <u>important quotes</u> and <u>examples</u> in your plan.

2) You could include them in a <u>table</u> like this one:

3) <u>Don't</u> spend <u>too long</u> writing out quotes though. It's just to make sure you <u>don't forget</u> anything when you write your answer.

A point...	Quote to back this up...
Another point...	Quote...
A different point...	Example...
A brand new point...	Quote...

Structure your answer

Introduction
↓
Middle Section
— paragraphs
expanding
your
argument.
↓
Conclusion

1) Your <u>introduction</u> should give a brief answer to the question you're writing about. Make it clear how you're going to <u>tackle the topic</u>.

2) The <u>middle section</u> of your essay should explain your answer in detail and give evidence to back it up. Write a <u>paragraph</u> for each point you make. Make sure you <u>comment</u> on your evidence and <u>explain how</u> it helps to <u>prove</u> your point.

3) Remember to write a <u>conclusion</u> — a paragraph at the end which <u>sums up</u> your <u>main points</u>. There's <u>more</u> about introductions and conclusions on the <u>next page</u>.

Dirk finally felt ready to tackle the topic.

To plan or not to plan, that is the question...

The answer is yes, yes, a thousand times yes. Often students dive right in, worried that planning will take up valuable time. But 5 minutes spent organising a well-structured answer is loads better than pages of waffle. Mmm waffles.

Writing Introductions and Conclusions

Now you've made that plan that I was banging on about on the last page, you'll know what your main points are. This is going to make writing your introduction and conclusion as easy as pie.

Get to the point straight away in your introduction

1) First, you need to work out what the question is asking you to do:

> How is the character of Simon important to the novel?

> The question is asking you to think about the role of Simon in the text.
> Plan your essay by thinking about how this character links to the text's overall message.

2) When you've planned your essay, you should begin by giving a clear answer to the question in a sentence or two. Use the rest of the introduction to develop this idea. Try to include the main paragraph ideas that you have listed in your plan, but save the evidence for later.

3) You could also use the introduction to give your opinion. Whatever you do, make sure your introduction makes it clear how your answer fits the question.

Your conclusion must answer the question

1) The most important thing you have to do at the end of your writing is to summarise your answer to the question.

2) It's your last chance to persuade the examiner, so make your main point again.

3) Use your last sentence to really impress the examiner — it will make your essay stand out. You could develop your own opinion of the text or highlight which of your points you thought was the most interesting.

The examiner was struggling to see the answer clearly.

Use the question words in your introduction and conclusion

1) Try to use words or phrases from the question in your introduction and conclusion.

> How does Golding use setting in the novel?

2) This will show the examiner that you're answering the question.

> Golding uses setting in 'Lord of the Flies' to create symbolic meaning. The island is used to reflect the characters' loss of innocence.

The first line of the introduction gives a clear answer, which will lead on to the rest of the essay.

3) This will also help you keep the question fresh in your mind so your answer doesn't wander off-topic.

I've come to the conclusion that I really like pie...

To conclude, the introduction eases the examiner in gently, whilst the conclusion is your last chance to impress. But remember — the examiner doesn't want to see any new points lurking in those closing sentences.

Writing Main Paragraphs

So we've covered the beginning and the end, now it's time for the meaty bit. The roast beef in between the prawn cocktail and the treacle tart. This page is about how to structure your paragraphs. It's quite simple...

P.E.E.D. is how to put your argument together

Remember to start a new paragraph every time you make a new point.

1) <u>P.E.E.D.</u> stands for: <u>P</u>oint, <u>E</u>xample, <u>E</u>xplain, <u>D</u>evelop.

2) Begin each paragraph by making a <u>point</u>. Then give an <u>example</u> from the text (either a quote or a description). Next, <u>explain</u> how your example backs up your point.

3) Finally, try to <u>develop</u> your point by writing about its effect on the reader, how it links to another part of the text or what the writer's intention is in including it.

Use short quotes to support your ideas

1) Don't just use words from the novel to show what <u>happens</u> in the <u>plot</u>...

> Jack becomes obsessed by hunting. He feels a "compulsion to track down and kill that was swallowing him up."

This just gives an example from the text without offering any explanation or analysis.

2) Instead, it's much better to use <u>short</u> quotes as <u>evidence</u> to support a <u>point</u> you're making.

3) It makes the essay structure <u>clearer</u> and <u>smoother</u> if most quotes are <u>embedded</u> in your sentences.

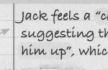

It's better to use short, embedded quotes as evidence. Then you can go on to explain them.

> Jack feels a "compulsion" to hunt and doesn't help Ralph to build the huts, suggesting that he's losing his civilised side. The need to hunt is "swallowing him up", which shows how his savage side is beginning to take over.

Get to know some literary language

1) Using <u>literary terms</u> in your answer will make your essay stand out — as long as you use them correctly.

2) When you're <u>revising</u>, think about literary terms that are <u>relevant</u> to the text and how you might <u>include</u> them in an essay. Take a look at the table below for some examples.

Literary Term	Definition	Example
Simile	Compares one thing to another, often using 'like' or 'as'.	Jack is "like a shadow" when he's hunting.
Foreshadowing	When the author hints at a future event.	Roger throws "a handful of stones" at Henry. Later, he uses a rock to kill Piggy.
Symbol	Something used by an author to represent something else.	The signal fire symbolises the boys' hope of being rescued.

This page is so exciting — I nearly...

Now now, let's all be grown-ups and avoid the obvious joke. It's a good way of remembering how to structure your paragraphs though. Point, Example, Explain, Develop. Simple. Maybe we could make a rap or something... anyone?

In the Exam

Keeping cool in the exam can be tricky. But if you take in all the stuff on this page, you'll soon have it down to a fine art. Then you can stroll out of that exam hall with the swagger of an essay-writing master.

Don't panic if you make a mistake

1) Okay, so say you've timed the exam beautifully. Instead of putting your feet up on the desk for the last 5 minutes, it's a good idea to <u>read through</u> your <u>answers</u> and <u>correct any mistakes</u>...

2) If you want to get rid of a mistake, <u>cross it out</u>. <u>Don't scribble</u> it out as this can look messy. Make any corrections <u>neatly</u> and <u>clearly</u> instead of writing on top of the words you've already written.

> techniques
> The author uses various literary ~~teknikues~~ to explore this theme .

> This is the clearest way to correct a mistake. Don't be tempted to try writing on top of the original word.

3) If you've <u>left out</u> a <u>word</u> or a <u>phrase</u> and you've got space to add it in <u>above</u> the line it's missing from, write the missing bit above the line with a '∧' to show exactly where it should go.

> Re-read the sentence carefully to work out where the '∧' symbol needs to go.

> and hyperbole
> The writer uses imagery to draw attention to this point.

4) If you've left out whole <u>sentences</u> or <u>paragraphs</u>, write them in a <u>separate section</u> at the <u>end</u> of the essay. Put a <u>star</u> (*) next to both the <u>extra writing</u> and the <u>place</u> you want it to go.

Always keep an eye on the time

1) It's surprisingly <u>easy</u> to <u>run out of time</u> in exams. You've got to leave <u>enough time</u> to answer <u>all</u> the questions you're asked to do. You've also got to leave enough time to <u>finish</u> each essay properly — with a <u>clear ending</u>.

2) Here are some <u>tips</u> on how to <u>avoid</u> running out of time:

- Work out <u>how much time</u> you have for each part of your answer <u>before</u> you <u>start</u>.

- Take off a few minutes at the beginning to <u>plan</u>, and a <u>few minutes</u> at the end for your <u>conclusion</u>.

- Make sure you have a <u>watch</u> to <u>time yourself</u> — and keep checking it.

- Be <u>strict</u> with yourself — if you spend <u>too long</u> on one part of your answer, you may run out of time.

- If you're <u>running out of time</u>, keep <u>calm</u>, <u>finish</u> the <u>point</u> you're on and move on to your <u>conclusion</u>.

Stephanie never had a problem with keeping cool.

Treat an exam like a spa day — just relax...

Some people actually do lose the plot when they get into the exam. The trick is to keep calm and well... carry on. If you make sure you get your exam technique sorted, you'll be as relaxed as a sloth in a room full of easy chairs.

Sample Exam Question

Now you've had a look at how to plan and structure your answer, it's time to see an example of how it can be done. The next three pages contain loads of useful bits and bobs like the very spidery spider diagram below.

Here's a sample exam question

Read this feisty exam question carefully...

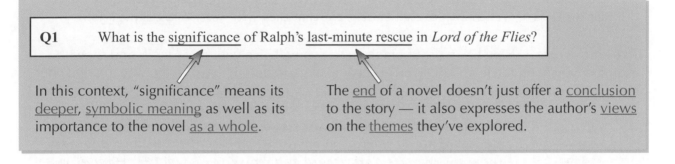

Q1 What is the <u>significance</u> of Ralph's <u>last-minute rescue</u> in *Lord of the Flies*?

In this context, "significance" means its <u>deeper</u>, <u>symbolic meaning</u> as well as its importance to the novel <u>as a whole</u>.

The <u>end</u> of a novel doesn't just offer a <u>conclusion</u> to the story — it also expresses the author's <u>views</u> on the <u>themes</u> they've explored.

Here's how you could plan your answer...

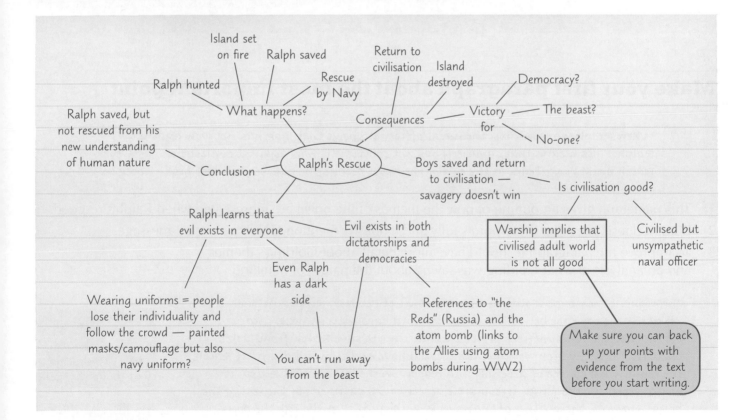

What do examiners eat? Why, egg-sam-wiches of course...

The most important thing to remember is DON'T PANIC. Take a deep breath, read the question, read it again, write a plan... take another deep breath... and then start writing. Leave about five minutes at the end to check your work too.

Worked Answer

These pages will show you how to take an okay answer and turn it into one that will really impress the examiner.

Use your introduction to get off to a good start

These pages are all about how to word your sentences to impress the examiner, so we haven't included everything from the plan on page 59.

1) You might <u>start</u> with something like...

> Ralph's last-minute rescue at the end of 'Lord of the Flies' is significant because it shows that the boys are returning to civilisation, but that they will never be the same again.

2) This intro is <u>okay</u>. Using key words from the <u>question</u> will give your essay <u>focus</u> and show the examiner you're on track, and that you're keeping the <u>question in mind</u> all the way through your essay.

3) But there's still room for <u>improvement</u> — it's a good idea to include a bit of <u>background</u> or <u>context</u>.

This intro talks about the context of the novel — what type, or genre, of book it is.

> On the surface, the last-minute rescue at the end of 'Lord of the Flies' is typical of many traditional adventure stories: after thrilling escapades, the main characters are rescued and return to normal life. However, on a deeper level Golding uses 'Lord of the Flies' to challenge the message of traditional adventure stories. The ending shows that although the boys are returning to civilisation, they will never be the same again.

This tells the examiner what the essay's about and shows that you've thought about your essay structure.

Make your first paragraph about the most important point

> When Ralph is rescued by the naval officer, it shows that Jack has not won against Ralph. This means that savagery has not completely won against civilisation. However, Ralph bursts into tears at the end of the novel because he realises he's lost his innocence.

1) This paragraph gives an <u>outline</u> of how the <u>themes</u> of the novel are represented when Ralph's <u>rescued</u>.

2) But... it doesn't <u>develop</u> these points <u>fully</u> and it doesn't mention Golding's overall message.

3) To improve the paragraph it should have more <u>detail</u> about Golding's themes and an <u>analysis</u> of what Golding was saying about the <u>nature of mankind</u>.

> Throughout the novel, Golding uses the conflict between Ralph and Jack to represent the conflict between civilisation and barbarity in man's nature. At the end, the naval officer arrives just in time to save Ralph from Jack's barbaric "hunt", which would undoubtedly have ended in his death. If Ralph, the remaining source of decency and reason on the island, was killed, it would represent the final, irreversible descent into savagery of the rest of the boys. However, the ending of the novel is ambiguous. Although the boys return to civilisation, the symbolism of the "burning wreckage of the island" shows how savage they have become. Golding is showing that the "beast" that terrorised them is part of human nature and they cannot escape from it. This evil is shown through the murders of Piggy and Simon; in contrast to the classic adventure story, good does not triumph over evil.

This is a nice introduction — it shows the examiner that you understand the themes of the novel.

Use the proper technical terms for things.

Show the examiner that you're aware of the message Golding was trying to get across.

Worked Answer

You need to make a variety of points

1) After you've talked about the <u>theme</u> of civilisation and barbarity, you might make a <u>second point</u> like this:

> It is ironic that the boys are rescued by a naval officer because he represents civilisation, but is fighting a barbaric war of his own. His clean white uniform contrasts with the boys' appearance.

2) It puts *Lord of the Flies* in its <u>context</u> — Golding wanted to comment on the barbarity of <u>war</u>.

3) However, you can make this paragraph better by giving more <u>detail</u> and backing up points with <u>quotes</u>.

> It is ironic that civilisation is represented by a military man, as his world of war and violence is merely the grown-up version of the boys' behaviour. His clean white uniform makes Ralph "conscious of his filthy appearance", which suggests that a uniform is a symbol of authority and society. However, like the uniform of face paint worn by the tribe, the officer's uniform allows him to lose his individuality and commit violent acts against other people.

Keep your quotes short and snappy.

Talking about Golding's use of symbolism shows that you've thought about the deeper meaning of the novel.

4) You could also <u>develop</u> it by describing how Golding uses the <u>viewpoint</u> of the naval officer:

Talking about how Golding uses different techniques like language and viewpoint will make your essay stand out.

> The arrival of the naval officer also allows Golding to show what the boys look like from an adult's perspective. During the hunt, Ralph sees them as "savages" with "spears" but the officer only sees "little boys" with "sharp sticks". This reinforces Golding's message that evil exists in everyone — even people who appear innocent.

Finish your essay in style

1) Always leave enough <u>time</u> to write a <u>conclusion</u>, like this:

> In conclusion, Ralph's last-minute rescue at the end of 'Lord of the Flies' is significant because the boys have lost their "innocence" and become savages. The naval officer's "revolver" and warship show that the grown-up world is savage too.

2) This is okay but it doesn't clearly explain Golding's <u>message</u> about the <u>nature</u> of mankind's evil.

3) So to make it really <u>impressive</u> you could say something like this:

> In conclusion, the true significance of the last-minute rescue is that Ralph hasn't been rescued at all. Although on the surface it appears that the boys have been saved, Ralph now recognises "the end of innocence" and "the darkness of man's heart". Despite being rescued from the savagery of the island, there is no escape from the savagery within man.

Make your last sentence really stand out — it's your last chance to impress the examiner.

Why do alligators write good essays? Their quotes are so snappy...

It seems like there's a lot to remember on these two pages, but there's not really. To summarise — write a good intro and conclusion, make a good range of points (one per paragraph) and put your most important point first. Easy.

Index

A

adventure stories 7, 17, 26, 29, 43, 50
America 48
animal imagery 17
appearance 22, 35
assemblies 6, 7, 9, 10, 34
atmosphere 7, 16, 20, 36, 38, 45
atom bomb 6, 48

B

barbarity 8-10, 12, 15, 17, 20-25,
          27-30, 34, 35
beast 7, 10-15, 26, 29, 30, 36, 40, 43
Beelzebub 40
boulders 11, 28, 39
British Empire 49
bullying 22

C

cake 6
Castle Rock 11, 16, 20, 23
chanting 34, 44
chief 6, 10, 11, 13, 23-25, 28, 39
choir 6, 24, 40, 49
civilisation 8-10, 12, 14, 15, 17,
          20-25, 27-30, 34, 35, 44, 45
Cold War 48
conch 6, 7, 10, 13-16, 20, 22, 34, 45
conclusions 56, 61
conflict 6, 9, 16, 50
The Coral Island 50

D

dancing 14, 29, 30, 38, 39
darkness 9, 12-14, 40
dead airman 11, 12, 14, 30, 48
democracy 7, 13, 16, 37, 45, 48
descriptive language 6, 12, 45
devil 40
dictatorship 13, 28, 37, 48

E

elections 6, 13, 39
evil 6, 13, 15-17, 20, 21, 25-28, 36,
          38, 40
exam advice 53-61
exploring 6, 43

F

fairness 7, 16, 20, 39
fear 6, 7, 10-12, 14, 15, 23, 24, 26, 29,
          30, 36, 40, 43, 48
feasts 14
fire 7-9, 15, 17, 24, 38, 45, 48
fruit 8, 22, 38
fun 7, 10, 13, 14, 34, 35, 37, 39
foreshadowing 10, 11, 15, 20, 25, 36,
          39, 45, 57

G

games 11, 12, 22, 29, 39
Garden of Eden 6, 38
general public 29
glasses 9, 15, 16, 22, 26, 34, 39, 50
good 13, 26, 27, 36, 38, 40
grown-ups 6, 17, 21, 22, 29, 30, 39, 43, 44, 50

H

hair 9, 10, 22, 43
Himmler 48
historical background 1, 2, 48, 49
Hitler 37, 48
human nature 17, 30, 36, 40, 48
hunting 6, 8-12, 17, 24, 25, 34, 40

I

identities 30, 45
imagery 17, 45
innocence 17, 21, 38, 44, 45
intelligence 22
introductions 56, 60
irony 17, 26, 34
island 6, 13, 38, 48, 50

J

Jack 6-16, 21, 23-25, 28, 29, 34-37, 39,
          43-45, 48-50
Jesus 27

L

lagoon 6, 38, 39
language 16, 44, 45
law and order 20
leadership 7, 8, 11-13, 23, 24, 28, 29, 36, 37
littluns 7, 10, 23, 29, 34
logic 23, 36
Lord of the Flies 13, 26, 27, 40
loyalty 23, 30, 48

M

masks 9
Maurice 9, 30
meat 8, 14, 26, 34, 37
mountain 6, 12
murders 14, 15, 27, 35, 43, 45

N

names 16, 22, 29, 30, 34, 45
nature 6, 8, 9, 12-14, 22, 27, 38
naval officer 13, 17, 30, 39, 40, 43, 44
Nazis 48
nightmares 29, 40
nuclear war 6, 36, 48

P

painted faces 9, 25, 30, 35
paradise 6, 38
pathetic fallacy 27

Percival 29
pigs 6, 8, 12, 13, 17, 22, 27, 28, 30, 50
Piggy 6, 7, 9, 10, 14-16, 20-27, 34, 36, 39,
          43-45, 48, 49
planning 55, 59
plane crash 6, 48
power 7, 9-14, 23, 24, 28, 29, 37
pride 23- 25
prophecies 12
public schoolboys 44, 49

R

Ralph 6-17, 20-23, 34-37, 39, 40, 43-45,
          48, 50
re-enactments 9, 12
rescue 8, 9, 20, 24, 34, 35, 37, 45, 59-61
responsibility 15, 20, 21, 29, 34, 35, 37, 44
Roger 9, 12, 28, 34, 35, 40, 48
rules 7, 10, 14, 16, 24, 34, 37
Robert 12, 30

S

Sam and Eric 11, 30, 48
sand castles 9, 28-30, 39
savagery 10, 12, 13, 17, 28-30, 34, 35,
          43, 45
shame 9, 20, 30
sharks 38
shelters 8, 10, 13, 14, 24, 34
ships 9, 17
similes 57
Simon 8-10, 12-15, 20, 24, 26, 27, 35, 36,
          38, 40, 43, 45
snake 7, 29
social class 49
storms 14, 38
structure 43
superstitions 13
swearing 44
symbolism 7, 9, 13, 15-17, 22, 27, 30, 34,
          36-38, 45, 57

T

time 43
torture 28, 30
tribe 13-17, 24, 25, 30, 35, 36, 39, 40, 43

U

uniforms 8, 10, 30, 35, 40, 49
USSR 48

V

viewpoints 43
violence 9, 13-15, 21, 25, 28, 34, 35, 37,
          39, 44, 48
voting 13, 24, 25, 28, 39

W

war 17, 30, 35, 36, 39, 43, 48
weather 27, 38
worked exam answer 60-61
World War II 48

The Characters from 'Lord of the Flies'

Phew! You should be an expert on *Lord of the Flies* by now. But if you want a bit of light relief and a quick recap of the novel's plot sit yourself down and read through *Lord of the Flies — The Cartoon*...

Ralph

Jack

Piggy

Simon

Roger

Sam and Eric

The dead airman

The 'littluns'

The 'Lord of the Flies'

William Golding's 'Lord of the Flies'